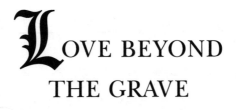

LOVE BEYOND THE GRAVE

LOVE BEYOND THE GRAVE

True Cases of Ghostly Lovers

HANS HOLZER

**BARNES
&NOBLE
BOOKS**
NEW YORK

This edition published by Barnes & Noble, Inc.,
by arrangement with Hans Holzer.

1992 Barnes & Noble Books

ISBN 0-88029-852-9

Printed and bound in the United States of America

M 9 8 7 6 5 4 3 2 1

CONTENTS

INTRODUCTION

EVER SINCE the successful motion picture *Ghost* stirred the imagination and curiosity of millions of people all over the world, the question of romantic ties beyond physical death has become one that can be discussed seriously even among those who would have laughed at such possibilities a scant ten years ago. But enough people saw this film to make it one of the highest-grossing movies in America, and questions about its validity from the general—often unconvinced—public are often far more intense, more searching, more positive in tone than, for example, questions about the validity of Oliver Stone's *JFK*.

Western society has been brainwashed for centuries by organized religion to "let well enough alone"—to give unto the world that which concerns the body, and give unto the church what concerns the soul, or whatever remains of the body after death. People in some

Eastern countries are less hostile to the notion of a real hereafter, though not necessarily for scientific reasons. Religions assume there is another world waiting when you leave this one, but look askance on any direct attempt to find out what it is like. Leaving that intelligence-gathering and, alas, interpretation to the clergy is rarely very helpful: at best it will give a partisan glimpse of that next dimension into which we all must pass; at worst a distorted, even frightening view of what lies ahead. The truth of the matter is that we already have so much hard evidence, from scientifically valid sources, regarding the next state of existence that one need not live one's life in ignorance and fear.

To understand how love and romance, and even sex, can exist between people in the physical world and those who are no longer in it, one should first come to understand the very nature of life itself. Only then does continuing communication, continuing bonds, with those on the "Other Side" make sense. In the final analysis, the nature of deep emotional relationships within the framework of the existing universe we know will become clearer. It does not mean we will have all the answers, but by examining our true nature we will be able to deal with such incidents properly—with neither fear nor with fanatic passion, but naturally, as each and every situation requires.

Hans Holzer, Ph.D.
New York, 1992

THE TRIPLE NATURE OF MAN

epending on your outlook, man is either a physical being with a puzzling, invisible extra called mind, and definitely a soul only on Sunday in church (but not really), or he is a triune of physical body, invisible but powerful mind force, and definitely soul, spirit, psyche—whichever term you prefer. The "three faces of man" are nothing like the *Three Faces of Eve,* the account of a bizarre case of multiple personality. Man's three faces are but different manifestations of a unit, each meant to function in certain ways and no other. To deny the existence of one of these aspects, or to denigrate its importance, leads to an incomplete understanding of the nature of man. And *that* lies at the bottom of so much of our troubles in this materialistically inclined age.

Although the "human machine" is far superior in concept to anything man has ever devised, it is still built upon natural law under which certain effects are due to certain causes, and some effects due to acausal but nevertheless valid and real relationships. In the eyes of the materialist, the machine called man is simply a well-functioning organism, depending on the continuing performance of its parts. When one or the other part deteriorates, the machine comes apart and malfunctions, and eventually man dies.

The progressive idealist sees man as a duality, in which a physical machine—the body—is joined and controlled by a mental force, which, however, is dependent on the body for its continued well-being and existence. When body dies, so does mind. In acknowledging that an invisible force called mind could have actual reality, the progressive idealist has already come a long way from the materialistic point of view, but he is equally distant from the full truth concerning the nature of man.

Only the esoteric thinker sees man as a whole, acknowledging freely that mind does not dissipate when body disintegrates, but on the contrary can have an existence of its own beyond and apart from the physical shell. In addition, the esoteric person accepts the existence of the soul, or psyche, or spirit, as the eternal factor in human life. The psyche continues its existence not only beyond bodily death but also beyond personality into another human form through the process of reincarnation.

With rare exceptions, the medical fraternity sees the human being as dualistic, treats the body or its parts rather than the whole, and refuses to accept the overwhelming evidence for the existence of the third force called psyche in scientific terms. The exceptions include such physicians as Dr. William McGarey of the Edgar Cayce Clinic in Phoenix, Arizona, who sees the body as *functional* rather than *structural:* The physical is simply an expression of the underlying spiritual element in man, which governs it, and not the other way around. Consequently the Cayce method (and all other forms of esoteric healing) treat the person as a whole, regardless of whether only a certain organ or part of the body is involved in illness or malfunction. By treating man, the affected part must also become well. For the esoteric physician, the existence of the psyche is further manifested by the human aura, first discovered (at least for our age) by Dr. Walter Killner in England over sixty years ago. Recently, experiments with so-called Kirlian photography (in which electric charges are used to make the "life force" visible to the camera) have added strong evidence for the existence in all living beings of an "inner self," a forcefield that contains not only the life force but also the essence of individuality in personality.

The outer layer—the physical body—responds to the environment through its five principal sensory organs, and initiates action through them in return. But it would not be able to do this without the help of the mind, which receives information through its nervous system, correlates it, and, through its nerve center in the brain, operates the body according to the impulses received.

The third layer of consciousness—the psyche—makes use of both of these systems, but is superior to them by virtue of greater knowledge, *cognizance,* drawn from both external and internal sources. The external input involves a linkup with the "deity force" and universal law administering it, and the internal supply of data comes from the deep recesses of the unconscious, the gateway to psychic awareness.

When the three layers are in harmony, man is well

and functions at maximum efficiency. When one or another layer is off balance, the entire system suffers.

How the physical body and mind work is the province of the physician and healer; suffice it to say here that I consider nearly all illness the result not of invasion of external forces or impurities but the imbalance in the system caused by disharmony from within. As man thinketh, so he feels. As man feels, so he will manifest. As he manifests, so he appears to the environment. Emotional thinking (not logical dissection) is at the root of all well-being.

Today we distinguish with painful arbitrariness where the precincts of medicine begin and end and where the province of the minister and priest lies. And yet, what is the difference between the counsel of the psychoanalyst and the minister or rabbi? Or, for that matter, the consulting medium or even the lowly fortune-teller? Are they not all catering to the same need of restoring harmony in the individual? Though their backgrounds and paths differ, their goal is the same.

Primitive man, and even civilized man until very recently, had no such choice of avenues. Medicine, religion, and even law were firmly interlinked and integrated one with the other; in seeking counsel man had to consider the problem from all these aspects, inseparably and indivisibly. The very system of life under which he existed was based upon this approach, and any attempt to separate one aspect from another was tantamount to heresy.

"In the beginning was the word," Goethe's Dr. Faust quotes the Bible. This literary character is merely the poet's spokesman for the eternal quest in man to find his place in the universe and, above all, his relation to the spiritual. What exactly *was* in the beginning? And what came before the beginning and who said, "Begin"? Questions like these have arisen in the minds of men ever since man breathed the air of this planet for the first time. Even among those who believe that God has created this world we live in, there are moments when they wonder when God began and who was there before Him. To say that chaos reigned prior to God's existence merely begs the issue by transferring the question onto another level of verbal expression. What, then, is chaos? And what preceded the chaos? Clearly, the question for the *ultimate* continues in the minds of believers and skeptics alike. In science, only parapsychology has made some tentative efforts toward exploring the question of the ultimate creator and the beginning of it all. But even here the question remains largely unanswered.

Anthony Borgia, in his work *Life In the World Beyond*, allegedly dictated by a deceased monsignor who found things different from what he himself had taught on the earth plane, speaks of the monsignor's quest for the *ultimate* once he arrived on the Other Side of life. But again the psyche is frustrated. Although he rises from plane to plane of existence, and learns more and more of the esoteric truth of the universe, he fails to come in contact with the ultimate and remains a questioner to the last.

From the dawn of history, man has sought to understand the omnipotent power around him that seems so much greater than himself. What he fails to understand, he worships—man *worships that which he cannot grasp intellectually.*

The process of worshiping a power greater than one's self, no matter what its nature might be, is expressed through *religious experience.* Something has to pass from physical man to the nonphysical deity concept: religious expression. The word *religion* first of all means to reaffirm one's ties, presumably with the deity. But the very word assumes that this tie has already been established somewhere in the distant past. And so it has. In falling to one's knees when worshiping the deity, one automatically accepts the fact that the deity was there before oneself. One assumes, therefore, that in worshiping it one merely does what one's antecedents did before, and thus *reaffirms* the ties established sometime in the past.

To *modern man,* doing something "religiously" means to do it according to the rules, to apply oneself completely and with the best of one's abilities. If we speak of a person as being religious, we consider that person possessed of a moral and spiritual code that perhaps others do *not* follow. If someone is frightened by an event and suddenly "gets religion," we refer to his improved responsibility. To the average meat eater, a vegetarian is an oddball with a kind of "personal religion" that forbids him to eat meat. Thus, religion also becomes synonymous with idiosyncracy, a personal code or even fetishism in today's usage.

In the country club set, no matter how much progress we make toward tolerance, a person's religion is still a guideline telling management whether or not the potential new member will "fit in" with the majority. We don't have information sheets requiring one to state one's religion every time one applies for a job or a club membership because that sort of thing is now frowned upon. But it persists just the same in more subtle and indirect ways, like it or not. The same hotels that used to advertise "Christian clientele" to keep Jewish people out now use half their advertising lineage to acquaint their prospective guests with the important fact that Protestant and Catholic churches *are nearby,* as if that were of the greatest importance to a vacationer. If you have national ambitions in political circles, being a Roman Catholic is still considered less desirable than being a Protestant.

What these people are talking about when they refer to a person's religious "affiliation" is of course not his spiritual attachment to the deity but merely the cubbyhole into which he will fit. The more conventional and majority-oriented that particular pew is, the more welcome the new person will be. But if we go back to the very *origins* of religion we will find far different connotations of this word.

Today we freely interchange the term *religion* with *faith* (What religion are you? What faith is he?). But originally they were not synonymous. A man's faith is a personal, subjective thing, something within to which only he can properly understand and relate. Faith need not necessarily be only religious. Faith in one's mission, one's abilities, in another person, an idea—these are all part of man's overall "faith." Religion, on the other hand, is the formal relationship with the power that governs the universe, whatever that power may be.

To have faith requires nothing more than an attitude. Faith can be entirely silent and exist only within the confines of man's thoughts. Religion, however, requires more than an attitude toward the deity. It requires practice and action, both to affirm that position and to strengthen the ties with the Supreme Power. Thus, the term *religion* should be understood more as an attempt on man's part to have proper ties with the

Higher Power than as a display or demonstration of personal convictions. There would not have been any religious feelings at all had man not always known that there was some power greater than himself to which he had to relate. Had he been born a Marxian Communist at the very beginning, and known only dialectic materialism, perhaps the need to have a relationship with the deity might not have developed. Instead, he would have made that very materialism his deity and worshiped it as a superpower. It is inherent within man to seek out a power greater than himself to have recourse to, especially when troubled. Man is aware, though often only dimly, of his own frailty and imperfection in relation to nature around him.

But if man was not born a materialist, as what then? Is man the sudden product of a willful Creator whose image we see, albeit imperfectly reflected, in the human species? Was he put on this planet earth by a *fiat,* a sudden decision, *a personal act* of an intelligence greater than man? If God, as an intelligent superpower, was out there somewhere in space, creating man, then surely He, in His infinite wisdom, would have wanted us to be sure of this fact. *But we are not;* some of us accept it on blind faith, as a tenet of a particular religious denomination, while others reject the notion as unscientific and illogical.

But if a personal deity did not create man in one fell swoop, surely *a great law* operating in the universe around us, of which we are part, must have been governing man's appearance on this planet. Such a law must surely be the work of a power greater than ourselves, even if *we* are also part of this power.

The ultimate cannot be answered by man for himself unless his mind is also capable of grasping it. Therein lies the difficulty: *The part cannot be greater than the total.*

But if we work toward a better understanding of *the guiding principles of our universe,* and learn more and more of its secrets, we will ultimately get to know the deity *through it.* This is sure to come when man's mind is ready, but only a mind *spiritually attuned* to the natural rhythm of the universe can fully grasp its inner workings.

Man, God, and the universe are related to each other, no matter what one's viewpoint might be. The difference arises from the position each element occupies in the scheme of things. There is, first of all, the traditional view of formal religion. To the traditionalist, man, created in the image of the deity, is of course in the center of the universe. He is not the lord of the universe, but he is the lord's favorite creation and therefore belongs at the hub of things. Parallel with this thinking came the idea that the earth was at the center of the universe. Even as late as the seventeenth century Galileo had to foreswear his scientific views concerning the relative position of sun and earth. "I don't want to be in the outer reaches of the universe, I want to be in the center of it," complained the cardinal conducting the inquisition of the famed scientist. Religious egotism no longer exists, but it seems to have been inherited by the orthodox *scientific establishment.*

Religion always recognized that man had a soul and a body: The body belonged to the earth, and must return to it, and the soul lent by God was properly God's, to be dealt with at the time of physical death. Deliberately, the religious establishments obscured the technical aspects of this duality so that man remained dependent upon its counsel.

Where modern parapsychology and religion differ is in the nature of the hereafter, and in the evaluation of man's psychic powers, both in the physical and in the nonphysical states.

Evidence for extrasensory perception and psychic phenomena goes back to the beginning of time. Men observed strange things they could not explain rationally and ascribed them to a deity. Among these phenomena were the ability to foretell the future and to have true dreams, and other forms of ESP such as healing and even telekinesis. Since primitive man could not account for these "extraordinary" happenings, he incorporated them into his religious faith. Whenever exceptions of natural law occurred, it was the will of the deity. Only God could circumvent the natural law; man could not.

Most of the so-called miracles of the past, or what appeared to be miracles to the contemporaries, were in fact plausible according to an extended view of natural law, such as we hold nowadays in psychic research. But at the time such an explanation was quite impossible, and the happenings *had* to be due to divine intercession, the suspension of the natural law for specific reasons known best to the Supreme Power. Seen from today's point of view, it appears incredible that so much of the religious establishment was built upon the observation of *seeming* miracles. This is the more remarkable as those responsible for the miracles were not even aware they were performing them. To them it was part of natural law, and though they might have felt themselves inspired by the deity, they were at no time acting as anything but human beings. Without the evidence of psychic phenomena, the religious establishment would not have a leg to stand on. Preciously little of the religious edifice, especially of the Western world, is built upon moral issues; much of it is based upon reports of a miraculous nature. Open-minded psychic researchers do not doubt the existence of another dimension into which everyone passes at the time of physical death. This nonphysical world is by no means the heaven of religion, just as, conversely, there does not seem to be any evidence whatever for the existence of a literal hell. But the evidential material from reliable sources, the large volume of experimental data accumulated by research groups, overwhelmingly supports the theory of this secondary dimension all around us. A large number of paranormal cases investigated by reputable researchers can be explained by extrasensory abilities on the part of flesh-and-blood people. That in itself is in contravention of orthodox scientific thinking, but it does not prove the existence of another dimension beyond the physical one. There remains, however, a very large body of material that can only be explained by the actual existence of another world in which human beings continue to function rationally and emotionally; in fact, very much as they did on the earth plane. The body of communications from this world, the larger number of observed apparitions and other forms of visual communications, is such that they simply cannot be explained away. There exists photographic material taken under test conditions supporting the theory of a nonphysical world, in the sense that we are in the midst of it at all times and merely exchange one density for another, as we pass from the physical into the spiritual world. Eastern religions in particular are closely linked with the concept of karma and reincarnation. Even Christianity had, at the very beginning, elements of reincarnation in its traditions, although they are no longer present in the later writings and practices. But most Eastern religions accept the existence of reincarnation fully and uncritically, even to the point of including transmigration of the soul, the possibility of man returning in the body of an animal. The law of karma is a universal and simple one. That which one does in one lifetime bears heavily upon one's circumstances in the next. Karma is made by a person himself. Depending upon his actions while in one life, he will either benefit or suffer in the next incarnation. There is no such thing as a punishing karma, something like a curse from one lifetime to another. Karma is merely the impersonal arbiter of human behavior and everyone is subject to this law. On the other hand, it gives man a chance to make up in another lifetime what he failed to do in a previous one, or a chance to set the record straight by being confronted with parallel conditions he failed to resolve properly before.

Naturally, man does not get any advance warnings what he is to do in the next lifetime should similar conditions occur. The whole concept of karma relies heavily on the inability of man to remember previous lives. Quite rightly so, for if we remember our past mistakes we could easily rectify them and there would be no particular merit to our efforts. Once in a while, man is permitted a glimpse of his past, nearly always where a lifetime has been cut short artificially, by accident, by tragedy, or in some violent way. Thus man gains a slight advantage from "remembering" bits and pieces of previous experiences and applying this knowledge to the present incarnation.

There is strong scientific evidence that reincarnation is a fact for all. Dr. Ian Stevenson of the University of Virginia, Charlottesville, has investigated the subject for many years. His work, *Twenty Cases Suggestive of Reincarnation,* is a standard text today. In my own book *Born Again—The Truth about Reincarnation,* I reported a number of cases that cannot be explained on any basis other than by reincarnation.

The question of karmic law versus free will has occupied not only the minds of Eastern philosophers but also of Western man, especially in recent years as Eastern philosophers have taken a stronger foothold in the Western world. If the karmic law is impersonal and always perfect, then there would be no room for free will. Free will, so dear to Western man, is of course also incompatible with the more orthodox religions of the Western world, since it is God's will that will be done, not man's. However, this basic conflict has been resolved in most religions by the insertion of prayer as an effective weapon to change God's will. The Easterner does the same, but accepts God's will beforehand, no matter what.

Seen from a scientific point of view, free will does have its limitations. There are numerous instances of precognition and clairvoyance pertaining to future events. If certain individuals can foresee events in great detail prior to their becoming objective reality and if these events are not merely generalities or happenings consistent with the law of chance, but to the contrary precise detailed and private events in people's lives, then the reality of foretelling the future cannot be disputed. In many instances events have been foreseen in great detail long before the individuals concerned were even born. Most noteworthy among the seers of the past was the French physician Nostradamus. He foresaw the assassination of French king Henry IV, on a highway, by a school teacher whose name he gave fully sixty years before the happening took place and many years before either principal was even born! The conclusion is that events exist independently of human beings, in another dimension where our concepts of time and space are apparently not operative. Whether events are created by the supreme deity and put in motion to test us, or whether some form of law is in operation in which fate and free will are related to each other, is difficult to assess without having first resolved the primary question of God and the universe. But the fact remains that events do exist prior to their becoming objective reality, prior to our being aware of them.

It seems to me then that free will is that effort on the part of individuals concerned that makes the best or the worst of any given event when it occurs. Depending upon our decision at the time of the event, we will either derive beneficial results from it or not. Consequently, we have a great deal of free will because it is up to us to decide what to do at any given moment when certain events occur in our lives. We do not have any control over the events themselves nor can we force them to occur or disappear. It is like a motorist on a highway: If he is a good driver, and if the road is in good condition, he will be able to make a fast decision when confronted with another car coming toward him on the same side of the road. Depending upon that split-second decision he will either have an accident or not, or the accident may be severe or not. The driver has no control over the condition of the road or the mechanical components of his car nor over the car coming toward him, but he does have control over his own reactions at the critical moment.

When a certain event occurs in one's life, one can take one of three positions. One can say, "Well, I've done the best and such and such has happened anyway" and blame oneself for not having done better. Or if the event is a happy one, one can be proud of one's wisdom in having made certain decisions and take full credit for the success. On the other hand, if one is less self-centered, one might accept God's will, whether the event is happy or tragic, and accept it as something that was *meant* to be, even though one really doesn't know why. The religious-oriented person will not quarrel with his God. He assumes that God knows best. In nearly all religions, the paternal attitude of the deity is assumed. Sometimes, God the Father is a taskmaster and acts more like a Dutch uncle than a benevolent creator. But man is always ready to explain that too by pointing at his sins, of which there are many at all times. There is, of course, the reincarnationist attitude, in which God's will is simply replaced by karma. The karmic law has meant it to be such and such and one's reactions were the kind that brought about certain results. If these results are not the best, then one is making up some past karma and that is all right too. If the results of one's efforts are negative, past bad karma is being straightened out. If the results are positive, one is being rewarded for some-

thing good done in a previous lifetime. Either way, the
karmic law is in operation and justice is being done.

But it seems to me that neither the blindly religious
attitude nor the *kismet* acceptance of the Eastern reincarnationist are exactly healthy attitudes toward the unknown. Both would gain if they were augmented by factual information concerning man's destiny and nature
derived from psychic research sources.

Dr. Joseph B. Rhine, pioneer in parapsychology
and originally a physiologist, said in a lecture in Boston:
"It is in the very nature of human organizations set up
to preserve and promote a set of doctrines, to become
resistant to innovations and to stop the very progressive
impulse that gave the organization its heritage. Nowhere more strikingly than in religious organizations,
the churches, does this stagnating resistance to change
manifest itself."

After assessing the generally negative attitude of established religious organizations toward any research
tending to prove *scientifically* the validity of religious
claims, Dr. Rhine adds: "The basic problem of all religion has been mentioned: the question of whether there
is anything spiritual in the universe. Every other conceivable problem concerning religion, great or small,
depends on an affirmative answer to this question."

Parapsychology has shown over the years that the
nonphysical element in man is indeed a reality and not
merely due to wishful thinking, or an illusion. "We can
safely conclude," Dr. Rhine continues, "that there is
something operative in man that transcends physical law
and, therefore, by definition, represents spiritual law.
The universe then is one about which it is possible to be
religious."

NEAR-DEATH EXPERIENCES: PROOF FOR A HEREAFTER

While it is true that the evidence for communication with the dead will present the bulk of evidential material for conditions and laws existing in that other world, we have also a number of testimonies from people who have entered the next world without staying in it. The cases involve people who were temporarily separated from their physical reality, without, however, being cut off from it permanently into the state we call death. These are mainly victims of accidents who recovered, people who underwent surgery and during the state of anesthesia had become separated from their physical bodies and were able to observe from a new vantage point what was being done to them, and in some instances people who traveled to the next world in a kind of dream-state and observed conditions there that they remembered upon returning to the full state of wakefulness. I hesitate to call these cases dreams since, as I have already pointed out in another work on the psychic side of dreams, the dream-state covers a multitude of conditions, some of which at least are not actual dreams but states of limited consciousness and receptivity to external inputs. Out-of-the-body experiences, formerly known as astral projections, are also frequently classed with dreams while in fact they are a form of projection in which the individual is traveling outside the physical body.

The cases I am about to present for the reality of this phenomenon have not been published before, and they are, to the best of my knowledge, true experiences by average individuals. I have always shied away from accepting material from individuals undergoing psychiatric care, not because I necessarily discount such testimony but because some of my readers might. As Dr. Raymond Moody noted in his work, there is a definite pattern in these near-misses, so to say, the experiences of people who have gone over and then returned. What they relate about conditions on the "other side of life" is frequently similar to what other people have said about these conditions, yet the witnesses have no way of knowing of each other's experiences, have never met, and have not read a common source from which they could draw such material if they were in a mood to deceive the investigator (which they certainly are not). In fact, much of this testimony is reluctantly given, out of fear of ridicule, or perhaps because the individual himself is not sure what to make of it. Far from the fanatical fervor of a religious purveyor, the individuals whose cases have been brought to my attention do not wish to convince anyone of anything, but merely to report to me what has occurred in their lives. In publishing these reports I am making the information available to those who might have had similar experiences and wondered about them.

We should keep in mind that the percipient of the experience would perceive entities and conditions in a three-dimensional way because he himself is three-dimensional in relation to the experience once he leaves his physical body. Thus it is entirely possible that an actual person would appear to the observer exactly the same way as a projection of a person would appear. If we accept the notion that the world beyond this one in which so-called spirit life continues is capable of creating by mind actual images of self as desired, even build houses by thought alone, yet is able to make them appear as solid and three-dimensional as people and houses are in this world, then the question of seeming contradictions to physical law as we know it is no longer such a puzzling one. Obviously an entity controlled by thought can pass through solid walls, or move at instantaneous speed from one place to another; during the temporary states between physical life and death, individuals partake of this ability and therefore undergo experiences that might otherwise be termed hallucinations. I cannot emphasize strongly enough that the cases I am reporting in the following pages do not fall into the category of what many doctors like to call hallucinations, mental aberrations, or fantasies. The clarity of the experiences, the full remembrance of it afterwards, the many parallels between individual experiences reported by people in widely scattered areas, and finally the physical conditions of the percipient at the time of the experience all weigh heavily against the dismissal of such experiences as being of hallucinatory origin.

Mrs. Virginia S., a housewife in one of the western states, has held various responsible jobs in management and business. On March 13, 1960, she underwent surgery for, as she put it, "repair to her muscles." During the operation she lost so much blood she was clinically dead. Nevertheless, the surgeons managed to bring her back and she recovered. This is what Mrs. S. experienced during the period when the medical team was unable to detect any sign of life in her.

"I was climbing a rock wall and was standing straight in the air; nothing else was around it, it seemed flat; at the top of this wall was another stone railing about two foot high. I grabbed for the edge to pull myself over the wall and my father, who is deceased, appeared and looked down at me. He said, 'You cannot come up yet, go back, you have something left to do.' I looked down and started to go down, and the next thing I heard were the words, 'She's coming back.' "

Mrs. J.L.H. is a housewife in her middle thirties who lives in British Columbia. Mrs. H. had an amazing experience on her way back from the funeral of her stepfather, George H. She was driving with a friend, Clarence G., and on the way there was a serious accident. Clarence was killed instantly, and Mrs. H. was seriously hurt. "I don't remember anything except seeing car lights coming at me, for I had been sleeping," Mrs. H. explained. "I first remember seeing my stepdad, George, step forward out of a cloudy mist and touch me on my left shoulder. He said, 'Go back, June, it's not yet time.' I woke up with the weight of his hand still on my shoulder."

The curious thing about this case is that both people were in the same accident, yet one of them was evidently marked for death while the other was not. After Mrs. H. had recovered from her injuries and returned home, she woke up one night to see a figure at the end of her bed holding out his hand toward her as if wanting her to come with him. When she turned her light on, the figure disappeared, but it always returned when she turned the light off again. During subsequent appearances, the entity tried to lift Mrs. H. out of her bed, ripping all the covers off her, forcing her to sleep with the lights on. It would appear that Clarence could not understand why he was on the other side of life while his friend had been spared.

Mrs. Phyllis G., who is from Canada, had a remarkable experience in March 1949. She had just given birth to twin boys in her own home, and the confinement seemed normal and natural. By late evening, however, she began to suffer from a very severe headache. By morning she was unconscious and was rushed to the hospital with a cerebral hemorrhage. She was unconscious for three days while the doctors were doing their best to save her life. It was during this time that she had her incredible experience.

"My husband's grandmother had died the previous August, but she came to me during my unconscious state, dressed in the whitest white robe, and there was light shining around her. She seemed to me to be in a lovely quiet meadow, her arms were held out to me, and she called my name, 'Phyllis, come with me.' I told her this was not possible as I had my children to take care of. Again she said, 'Phyllis, come with me, you will love it here.' Once again, I told her it wasn't possible. I said, 'Gran, I can't, I must look after my children.' With this she said, 'I must take someone. I will take Jeffrey.' I didn't object to this and Gran just faded away. Jeffrey is the first twin that was born." Mrs. G. recovered, and her son Jeffrey wasn't taken either, and is now a grown man and doing fine. However, his mother still has this nagging feeling in the back of her mind that perhaps his life may not be as long as it ought to be. During the time Mrs. G. saw her grandmother she had been thought clinically dead.

There are many cases on record where a person begins to partake of another dimension while there is still hope for recovery but the ties between consciousness and body are already beginning to loosen. An interesting case was reported to me by Mrs. J. P. of California. While still a teenager, Mrs. P. had been very ill with influenza, but was just beginning to recover when she had a most unusual experience. One morning her father and mother came into her bedroom to see how she was feeling. "After a few minutes I asked them if they could hear the beautiful music. I still remember that my father looked at my mother and said, 'She's delirious.' I vehemently denied that. Soon they left but as I glanced out my second-floor bedroom window toward the wooded hills I love, I saw a sight that literally took my breath away. There, superimposed on the trees, was a beautiful cathedral-type structure from which that beautiful music was emanating. Then I seemed to be looking down on the people. Everyone was singing, but it was the background music that thrilled my soul. A leader dressed in white was leading the singing. The interior of the church seemed strange to me. It was only in later years, after I had attended services in an Episcopal church and also in a Catholic church, that I realized the front of the church I saw was more in their style, with the beautiful altar. The vision faded. Two years later, when I was ill again, the scene and music returned."

On January 5, 1964, Mr. R.J.I. of Pittsburgh was

rushed to the hospital with a bleeding ulcer. On admittance he received a shot and became unconscious. Attempts were immediately made to stop the bleeding and finally he was operated on. During the operation, Mr. I. lost fifteen pints of blood, suffered convulsions and a fever of one hundred six degrees. He was as close to death as one could come and was given the last rites of his church. However, during the period of his unconsciousness he had a remarkable experience. "On the day my doctor told my wife I had only an hour to live, I saw while unconscious a man, with black hair and a white robe with a gold belt, come from behind an altar, look at me, and shake his head. I was taken to a long hall and purple robes were laid out for me. There were many candles lit in this hall."

Many cases of this kind occur when the subject is being prepared for surgery or while undergoing surgery; sometimes the anesthetic allows dissociation to occur more easily. This is not to say that people hallucinate under the influence of anesthetic drugs, or due to the lack of blood, or from any other physical cause. If death is the dissolution of the link between physical body and etheric body, it stands to reason that any loosening of this link is likely to allow the etheric body to move away from its physical shell, although still tied to it either by a visible silver cord or by some form of invisible tie that we do not as yet fully understand. Otherwise, those who have returned from the great beyond would not have done so. Mrs. J. M., a widow in her early fifties, mother of four children and a resident of Canada, was expecting her fourth child in October 1956.

"Something went wrong and when I had a contraction, I went unconscious. My doctor was called and I remember him telling me he couldn't give any anes-thetic as he might have to operate. Then I passed out, but I could still hear him talking and myself talking back to him. Then I couldn't hear him any longer and I found myself on the banks of a river with green grass and white buildings on the other side. I knew if I could get across I'd never be tired again, but there was no bridge and it was very rough. I looked back and I saw myself lying there with nurses and doctors around me, and Dr. M. had his hand on the back of my neck and he was calling me and he looked so worried that I knew I had to go back. I had the baby and then I was back in the room and the doctor explained to my husband what happened. I asked him why he had his hand on my neck and he replied that it was the only place on my body where he could find a pulse, and for over a minute he couldn't even feel one there. Was this the time when I was standing on the riverbank?"

Deborah B. is a young lady living in California with a long record of psychic experiences. At times when she's intensely involved in an emotional situation she undergoes what we parapsychologists call a dissociation of personality. For a moment she is able to look into another dimension, partake of visionary experiences not seen or felt by others in her vicinity. One such incident occurred to Deborah during a theater-arts class at school. She looked up from her script and saw "a man standing there in a flowing white robe, staring at me, with golden or blond hair, down to his shoulders; a misty fog surrounded him. I couldn't make out his face, but I knew he was staring at me. During this time I had a very peaceful and secure feeling. He then faded away." Later that year, after an emotional dispute between Deborah and her mother, another visionary experience took place. "I saw a woman dressed in a long blue flowing robe with a white shawl or veil over her head, beckoning to a group of three or four women dressed in rose-colored robes and white veils. The lady in blue was on the steps of a church or temple with very large pillars. Then it faded out." One might argue that Deborah's imagination was creating visionary scenes within her, if it weren't for the fact that what she describes has been described by others, especially people who have returned from the threshold of death. The beckoning figure in the flowing robe has been reported by many, sometimes identified as Jesus, sometimes simply as a Master. The identification of the figure depends, of course, on the religious or metaphysical attitude of the subject, but the feeling caused by his appearance seems to be universally the same—a sense of peace and complete contentment.

Mrs. C. B. of Connecticut has had a heart problem for over twenty-five years. The condition is under control so long as she takes the tablets prescribed for her by her physician. Whenever her blood pressure passes the two-hundred mark, she reaches for them. When her pulse rate does not respond to the medication, she asks to be taken to the hospital for further treatment. There drugs are given to her intravenously, an unpleasant procedure that she tries to avoid at all costs. But she has lived with this condition for a long time and knows what she must do to survive. On one occasion she had been reading in bed and was still awake around five o'clock in the morning. Her heart had been acting up again for an hour or so. She even applied pressure to various pressure points she knew in the hope that her home remedies would slow down her pulse rate, but to no avail. Since she did not wish to awaken her husband, she was waiting to see whether the condition would abate by itself. At that moment, Mrs. B. had a most remarkable experience. "Into my window flew or glided a woman. She was large, beautiful, and clothed in a multicolored garment with either arms or wings close to her sides. She stopped and hovered at the foot of my bed to the right and simply stayed there. I was so shocked and yet I knew that I was seeing her as a physical being. She turned neither to the right nor to the left but remained absolutely stone-faced and said not a word. Then I seemed to become aware of four cherubs playing around and in front of her. Yet I sensed, somehow, that these were seen with my mind's eye rather than with the material eyes. I don't know how to explain from any reasonable standpoint what I said or did, I only knew what happened. I thought, 'This is the angel of death. My time has come.' I said audibly, 'If you are from God, I will go with you.' As I reached out my hand to her, she simply vanished in mid-air. Needless to say, the cherubs vanished too. I was stunned, but my heart beat had returned to normal."

Mrs. L. L. of Michigan dreamed in July 1968 that she and her husband had been killed in an automobile accident. In November of that year, the feeling that death was all around her became stronger. Around the middle of the month, the feeling was so overwhelming she telephoned her husband, who was then on a hunting trip, and informed him of her death fears. She discussed her apprehensions with a neighbor, but nothing helped allay her fears. On December 17, Mrs. L. had still another dream, again about imminent death. In this dream she knew that her husband would die and that she could not save him, no matter what she did. Two days later, Mrs. L. and her husband were indeed in an automobile accident. He was killed and Mrs. L. nearly died. According to the attending physician, Dr. S., she should have been a dead woman, considering her injuries. But during the stay in the hospital when she had been given up, and was visited by her sister, she spoke freely about a place she was seeing and the dead relatives she was in contact with at the time. She knew that her husband was dead, but she also knew that her time had not come, that she had a purpose to achieve in life and therefore could not stay on the "plane" on which she was temporarily. The sister, who did not understand any of this, asked whether Mrs. L. had seen God, and whether she had visited heaven. The unconscious subject replied that she had not seen God nor was she in heaven, but on a certain plane of existence. The sister thought that all this was nonsense and that perhaps her dying sister was delirious. Mrs. L. herself remembers quite clearly how life returned to her after her visit to the other plane. "I felt life coming to my body, from the tip of my toes to the tip of my head. I knew I couldn't die. Something came back into my body, I think it was my soul. I was at complete peace about everything and could not grieve about the death of my husband. I had complete forgiveness for the man who hit us; I felt no bitterness toward him at all."

Do some people get an advance glimpse at their own demise? It would be easy to dismiss some of the precognitive or seemingly precognitive dreams as anxiety-caused, perhaps due to fantasies. However, many of these dreams parallel each other and differ from ordinary anxiety dreams in their intensity and the fact that they are remembered so very clearly upon awakening. A good case in point is a vivid dream reported to me by Mrs. Peggy C., who lives in a New York suburb. She had recently developed a heart condition and was wondering whether a dream she had had twenty years before was an indication that her life was nearing its end. The dream that had so unnerved her through the years had her walking past a theater where she met a dead brother-in-law. "I said to him, 'Hi, Charlie, what are you doing here?' He just smiled and then in my dream it dawned on me the dead come for the living. I said to him, 'Did you come for me?' He said, 'Yes.' I said to him, 'Did I die?' He said, 'Yes.' I said, 'I wasn't sick. Was it my heart?' He nodded, and I said, 'I'm scared.' He said, 'There is nothing to be scared of, just hold onto me.' I put my arms around him and we sailed through the air in darkness. It was not a frightening feeling but a pleasant sensation. I could see the buildings beneath us. Then we came to a room where a woman was at a desk. In the room was my brother-in-law, an old lady, and a mailman. She called me to her desk. I said, 'Do we have to work here too?' She said, 'We are all assigned to duties. What is your name?' I was christened Bernadine but my mother never used the name; I was called Peggy. I told her 'Peggy,' she said, 'No. Your name is Bernadine.' After taking the details, my brother-in-law took me by the arms and was taking me upstairs, when I awakened. I saw my husband standing over me with his eyes wide open, but I could not move. I was thinking to myself, 'Please shake me, I'm alive,' but I could not move or talk. After a few minutes, my body jerked in bed and I opened my eyes and began to cry." The question is, did Mrs. C. have a near-death experience and return from it, or was her dream truly precognitive, indicative perhaps of things yet to come?

Doctor Karlis Osis has published his findings concerning many deathbed experiences, wherein the dying recognize dead relatives in the room, seemingly come to help them across the threshold into the next world. A lady in South Carolina, Mrs. M. C., reported one particularly interesting case to me recently. She herself has a fair degree of mediumship, which is a factor in the present case. "I stood behind my mother as she lay dying at the age of some seventy years. She had suffered a cerebral stroke and at this particular time of her life she was unable to speak. Her attendants claimed they had had no communication with her for over a week previously. As I let my mind go into her, she spoke clearly and flawlessly. 'If only you could see how beautiful and perfect it all is,' she said, then called out to her dead father, saying 'Papa, Papa.' I then spoke directly to her and asked her did she see Papa? She answered as if she had come home, so to speak. 'Yes, I see Papa.' She passed over onto the other side shortly, in a matter of days. It was as if her father had indeed come after her as I had spoken with her when she saw him and spoke clearly despite paralyzed mouth and throat muscles."

Sometimes the dead want the living to know how wonderful is their newly found world. Whether this is out of a desire to make up for ignorance in one's earth life when such knowledge was either outside one's ken or ignored, or whether this is in order to acquaint the surviving relative with what lies ahead, cases involving such excursions into the next world tend to confirm the near-death experiences of those who have gone into it on their own, propelled by accidents or unusual states of consciousness. One of the most remarkable reports of this kind comes to me through the kindness of two sisters living in England. Mrs. Doreen Barker is a senior nursing administrator who has witnessed death on numerous occasions. Here is her report:

In May 1968 my dear mother died. I had nursed her at home during which time we had become extremely close. My mother was a quiet, shy woman who always wished to remain in the background. Her last weeks were ones of agony; she had terminal cancer with growths in many parts of her body. Toward the end of her life I had to sedate her heavily to alleviate the pain, and after saying good-bye to my daughter on the morning of the seventh of May, she lapsed into semiconsciousness and finally died in a coma, approximately 2:15 A.M. on the eighth of May, 1968. A few nights after her death I was gently awakened. I opened my eyes and saw Mother. Before I relate what happened I should like to say that I dream vividly every night and this fact made me more aware that I was *not* dreaming. I had not taken any drinks or drugs, though of course my mind and emotions revolved around my mother. After Mother woke me, I arose from my bed. My hand instinctively reached out for my dressing gown but I do not remember putting it on. Mother said that she would take me to where she was. I reacted by saying that I would get the car out, but she said that I would not need it.

We traveled quickly, I do not know how, but I was aware that we were in the Durking Leatherhead area and entering another dimension. The first thing

I saw was a large archway. I knew I had seen it before although it means nothing to me now. Inside the entrance a beautiful sight met my eyes. There was glorious parkland, with shrubbery and flowers of many colors. We traveled across the parkland and came to a low-built white building. It had the appearance of a convalescence home. There was a veranda, but no windows or doors as we know them. Inside everything was white and Mother showed me a bed that she said was hers. I was aware of other people but they were only shadowy white figures. Mother was very worried about some of them and told me that they did not know that they were dead. However I was aware that one of a group of three was a man. Mother had always been very frugal in dress, possibly due to her hardships in earlier years. Therefore her wardrobe was small but neat and she spent very little on clothing if she could alter and mend. Because of this I was surprised when she wished that she had more clothes. In life Mother was the kindest of women, never saying or thinking ill of anyone. I therefore found it hard to understand her resentment of a woman in a long flowing robe who appeared on a bridge in the grounds. The bridge looked beautiful but Mother never took me near it. I now had to return, but I was extremely distressed to hear, in response to my question 'Are you happy?' that she did not want to leave her family. Before Mother left me she said a gentle 'Goodbye, dear.' It was said with a quiet finality and I knew that I would never see her again.

It was only afterward when I related it to my sister that I realized that Mother had been much more

youthful than when she died and that her back, which
in life had been rounded, was straight. Also I realized
that we had not spoken through our lips but as if by
thought, except when she said, 'Goodbye, dear.' It is
three and a half years since this happening and I have
had no further experience. I now realize that I must
have seen Mother during her transition period when
she was still earth-bound, possibly from the effects of
the drugs I administered under medical supervision,
and when her tie to her family, particularly her
grandchild, was still very strong.

Patricia Nobel, sister to Mrs. Barker, kindly wrote
her own account of the incident, "separately and without consulting each other." As Mrs. Nobel remembers it,
her sister reported the incident to her shortly after it
occurred. "My sister told me that she felt herself being
gently shaken awake and when she opened her eyes, my
mother was bending over her. She was wearing ordinary dress and looked as she did some twenty-five years
earlier." Mrs. Nobel then goes on to confirm pretty
much what her sister had written to me. She adds, "She
told my sister she would not be staying where she was
but gave no indication as to where she was going. There
were no other buildings to be seen in this vast parkland
area. It otherwise appeared to be totally deserted and
exceptionally beautiful and peaceful. My deepest regret
is that my sister and I had never taken an interest in
ESP, spiritualism, or mediums up to that time and were
therefore totally unprepared for what happened."

Don McIntosh is a professional astrologer living in
Richland, Washington. Now in his early seventies, he
worked most of his life as a security patrolman, his last

employment being at an atomic plant in Washington
state. After retirement, he took up astrology full-time.
Though he had had no particular interest in psychic
phenomena, he had a remarkable experience that convinced him of the reality of afterlife existence.

"On November 15, 1971, at about six-thirty A.M., I
was beginning to awaken when I clearly saw the face of
my cousin near the foot of my bed. He said, 'Don, I have
died.' Then his face disappeared, but the voice was definitely his own distinctive voice. As far as I knew at that
time, he was alive and well. The thought of telling my
wife made me feel uncomfortable, so I did not tell her of
the incident. At 11 A.M., about four and a half hours after
my psychic experience, my mail arrived. In the mail was
a letter from my cousin's widow, informing us that he
had had a heart failure and was pronounced dead upon
arrival. She stated that his death occurred at 9:30 P.M.,
November 8, 1971, at Ventura, California. My home,
where my psychic experience took place, is at least a
thousand miles from Ventura, California. The incident
is the only psychic experience I've ever had."

William W. lives and works in Washington, D.C. Because of some remarkable psychic incidents in his life,
he began to wonder about survival of human personality. One evening recently he had a dream in which he
saw himself walking up a flight of stairs where he was
met by a woman whom he immediately recognized as
his elderly great-aunt. She had died in 1936. "However,
she was dressed in a gray long dress of the turn-of-the-
century style, her hair was black, and she looked vi-
brantly young. I asked her in the dream where the others were, and she referred me to a large room at the top
of the stairs. The surroundings were not familiar. I en-

tered the room and was amazed to see about fifteen people in various types of dress, both male and female and all looking like mature adults, some about the age of thirty. I was able to recognize nearly all of these people although most I had seen when they were quite old. All appeared jovial and happy. I awakened from the dream with the feeling that somebody had been trying to tell me something."

There are repeated reports indicating that the dead revert to their best years, which lie around the age of thirty in most cases, because they are able to project a thought-form of themselves as they wish. On the other hand, where apparitions of the dead are intended to prove survival of an individual, they usually appear as they looked prior to death, frequently wearing the clothes they wore at the time of their passing.

Not all temporary separations of body and etheric self include a visit to the next world. Sometimes the liberated self merely hangs around to observe what is being done with the body. Mrs. Elaine L., of Washington State, recently reported an experience that happened to her at the age of sixteen. "I had suffered several days from an infected back tooth, and since my face was badly swollen, our dentist refused to remove the tooth until the swelling subsided. Shortly after the novocaine was administered, I found myself floating close to an open window. I saw my body in the dental chair and the dentist working feverishly. Our landlady, Mrs. E., who had brought me to the dentist, stood close by, shaking me and looking quite flabbergasted and unbelieving. My feeling at the time was of complete peace and freedom. There was no pain, no anxiety, not even an interest in what was happening close to that chair. Soon I was back to the pain and remember as I left the office that I felt a little resentful. The dentist phoned frequently during the next few days for assurance that I was all right."

According to a recent report, a Trappist monk who had suffered a cardiac arrest for a period of ten minutes remembered a visit to a world far different from what his religion had taught him. Brother Gerard spoke of seeing fluffy white clouds and experiencing a sense of great joy. As a result of his amazing experience, the monk now helps people on the terminal list of a local hospital face death more adequately. He can tell them that there is nothing to fear.

A New Jersey physician, Dr. Joseph Guzik, recently admitted publicly that he had "died" after a severe attack of pneumonia in 1934 and could actually see himself lying on the deathbed. At the time he worried what his mother would say if he died, when he heard a voice tell him that it was entirely up to him whether he wanted to stay on the physical plane or go across. Because of his own experience, Dr. Guzik later paid serious attention to the accounts of several patients who had similar experiences.

There are a considerable number of cases involving near-death experiences, reports from people who were clinically dead for varying lengths of time and who then recovered and remembered what they experienced while unconscious. If we assume that universal law covers all contingencies, there should be no exceptions to it. Why then are some people allowed to glimpse what lies ahead for them in the next dimension without actually entering that dimension at the time of the experience? After investigating large numbers of such cases I can only surmise that there are two reasons. First of all, there must be a degree of self-determination involved, allowing the subject to go forward to the next dimension or return to the body. As a matter of fact, in many cases, though not in all, the person is being given that choice and elects to return to earth. Secondly, by disseminating these witnesses' reports among those in the physical world, knowledge is put at our disposal, or rather at the disposal of those who wish to listen. It is a little like a congressional leak, short of an official announcement and much more than a mere rumor. In the final analysis, those who are ready to understand the nature of life will derive benefits from this information, and those who are not ready, will not.

III

WAKING UP "DEAD," OR WHAT HAPPENED TO ME?

here are three kinds of contact between "discarnates"—people who have "died" and are in the next dimension—and those left behind in the physical world. Of course, those whose body has died are now in another, finer "inner" body and by no means just "nothing," or just a "thought form." They are usually in full control of their movements, even desires. But sometimes they don't realize that they have left their *physical* bodies behind, or what happened to them to cause their changed circumstances. This is the case I am reporting here.

The other two contacts are deliberate: the person on the "Other Side" of life desires to make contact with a living person in the physical world. Contact number two is mainly visual, a message that would identify the sender. Usually it is to let the family or friends know that they are well.

Then there is contact number three—physical contact. People who have experienced such contacts speak of them as if they had occurred between living people.

They can range, as we will see, from merely gently touching someone lovingly, to attempt at full sexual intercourse.

The first and second types of contact are not difficult to deal with, and they sometimes cease spontaneously. The third kind is far more complex. But here we deal with the first type.

Take the case of Mrs. G. A. in Santa Susana, for instance. Mrs. A. is not a person given to belief in the supernatural. In fact, her total disbelief that the events that shook her up in 1958 were in any way psychic caused her to contact me. Somehow the "rational" explanation—grief over the passing of her husband—did not satisfy her eager mind and ultimately she wanted to know.

Her husband and Mrs. A. were working on their boat in the backyard on a warm California day. Suddenly, she heard him cry out "Honey," as if in pain. He had been working with an electric sander at the time. Alarmed, Mrs. A. turned around in time to see him clutching the sander to his chest. He had been accidentally electrocuted. Quickly she pulled the electric plug out and tried to hold him up, all the while screaming for help, but it was too late.

The ironical part was that A. had had nightmares and waking fears about just such an accident—death from electrocution.

Two months went by and Mrs. A. tried to adjust to her widowhood. One night she was roused from deep sleep by "something" in the room. As soon as she was fully awake she perceived an apparition of her late husband, suspended in the air of their room. He did not make any sound or say anything. Strangely enough, the apparition wore no shirt; he was bare-chested, as he would not have been in life.

In a moment he was gone, and Mrs. A. went back to sleep. In the morning she convinced herself that it was just a case of nerves. The day wore on. It was 4:30 in the afternoon and Mrs. A. was seated on her living room couch, relaxing and waiting for a telephone call from her mother. All of a sudden, she heard her car drive up to the door. She realized at once that this could not be the case, since she was not driving it, but it struck her also that this was the precise time her husband always drove up to the door, every afternoon!

Before she could fully gather her wits, he was there in the room with her. He looked as he had always looked, not transparent or ethereal. Mrs. A. was literally frozen with fear. Her late husband knelt before her seemingly in great emotion, exclaiming, "Honey, what's wrong?"

At this point, Mrs. A. found her tongue again and, as quietly as she was able to, told her late husband what had happened to him.

"There was an accident, and you were killed."

When she had said those words, he uttered the same sound he did at the time of the accident—"Honey!"—as if remembering it—and instantly he vanished.

Mrs. A. has never felt him around her again since. Evidently, her husband has adjusted to his new state.

IV

ROMANCE UNFINISHED: WHEN THE GHOSTLY LOVER MAKES CONTACT

When one half of a couple passes out of the physical world, the half left behind will grieve and, eventually, get over it, even find another romantic partner. That is as it should be, though grieving for someone who has gone on is not helpful either to the one left behind or to the one who has gone on, as it will affect them adversely.

Attentions from the dead lover often are not encouraged from the side of the living partner. Occasionally the bond is still so strong that it is accepted, even desired, though this harbors great dangers in some cases, ranging from psychological damage to the possibility of induced possession.

An elderly Canadian lady had divorced her husband long before he died, but immediately he was "over there," he started contacting her and making every effort to continue what he still perceived as a relationship. She did not want it—she had not wanted it before he died and wanted it even less afterwards, but he persisted and caused her much anguish, until we were finally able to break his hold on her psyche, at least to the extent that she was able to control his incursions.

When people pass over to the Other Side, nothing in their character changes immediately; their unfulfilled desires are as strong as before. They will try to get back to their usual surroundings, their old homes, and impress their companions with their presence. Depending on the degree of the living person's psychic abilities, it will work well, badly, or not at all. But it is rarely frightening or dangerous to the living.

Mrs. J. H. is a housewife living in Maryland. At the time of these incidents her son Richard was seven and her daughter Cheryl, six. Hers was a conventional marriage until the tragic death of her husband, Frank. On September 3, he was locking up a restaurant where he was employed near Washington, D.C. Suddenly two men entered by the rear door and shot him during an attempted robbery. For more than a year after the murder, no clue as to the murderers' identities was found by the police.

Mrs. H. was still grieving over the sudden loss of her husband when something extraordinary took place in her home. Exactly one month to the day after his death, she happened to be in her living room when she saw a "wall of light" and something floated across the living room toward her. From it stepped the person of her late husband. He seemed quite real to her, but somewhat transparent. Frightened, the widow turned on the lights and the apparition faded.

From that moment on, the house seemed to be alive with strange phenomena: knocks at the door that disclosed no one who could have caused them, the dog barking for no good reason in the middle of the night, or the cats staring as if they were looking at a definite person in the room. Then one day the two children went into the bathroom and saw their dead father taking a shower! Needless to say, Mrs. H. was at a loss to explain that to them. The widow had placed all of her late husband's clothes into an unused closet that was kept locked. She was the last one to go to bed at night and the first one to arise in the morning, and one morning she awoke to find Frank's shoes in the hallway; nobody could have placed them there.

One day Mrs. H.'s mother, Mrs. D., who lives nearby, was washing clothes in her daughter's basement. When she approached the washer, she noticed that it was spotted with what appeared to be fresh blood. Immediately she and the widow searched the basement, looking for a possible leak in the ceiling to account for the blood, but they found nothing. Shortly afterward, a sister of the widow arrived to have lunch at the house. A fresh tablecloth was placed on the table. When the women started to clear the table after lunch, they noticed that under each dish there was a blood spot the size of a fifty-cent piece. Nothing they had eaten at lunch could possibly have accounted for such a stain.

But the widow's home was not the only place where manifestations took place. Her mother's home was close by, and one night a clock radio alarm went off by itself in a room that had not been entered by anyone for months. It was the room belonging to Mrs. H.'s grandmother, who had been in the hospital for some time before.

It became clear to Mrs. H. that her husband was

trying to get in touch with her, since the phenomena continued at an unabated pace. Three years after his death, two alarm clocks in the house went off at the same time though they had not been set, and all the kitchen cabinets flew open by themselves. The late Frank H. appeared to his widow punctually on the third of each month, the day he was murdered, but the widow could not bring herself to address him and ask him what he wanted. Frightened, she turned on the light, which caused him to fade away. In the middle of the night Mrs. H. would feel someone shake her shoulder, as if to wake her up. She recognized this touch as that of her late husband, for it had been his habit to wake her in just that manner.

Meanwhile the murderers were caught. Unfortunately, by one of those strange quirks of justice, they got off very lightly, one of the murderers with three years in prison, the other with ten. It seemed like a very light sentence for having taken a man's life so deliberately.

Time went on, and the children were ten and eleven years of age, respectively. Mrs. H. could no longer take the phenomena in the house and moved out. The house was rented to strangers who are still living in it. They have had no experiences of an uncanny nature since, after all, Frank wants nothing from *them*.

As for the new house where Mrs. H. and her children live now, Frank has not put in an appearance as of yet. But there are occasional tappings on the wall, as if he still wanted to communicate with his wife. Mrs. H. wishes she could sleep in peace in the new home, but then she remembers how her late husband, who had

been a believer in scientology, had assured her that
when he died, he would be back. . . .

The Ghostly Lover need not be half of a married couple, or even one of two unmarried people who used to
live together. Even a relationship that had been strong
in life (at least on the part of one of the people involved)
but had never been consummated can cause a problem
between the Two Worlds. When the desire to have a
relationship is so strong even after death, an attempt
may yet be made to make it happen!

Grace Rivers was a secretary by profession, a lady of
good background, and not given to hallucinations or
emotional outbursts. I had spoken with her several
times and always found her most reluctant to discuss
what to her seemed incredible.

It seemed that on weekends, Miss Rivers and another secretary, by the name of Juliet, were the house
guests of their employer, John Bergner, in Westbrook,
Connecticut. Miss Rivers was also a good friend of this
furniture manufacturer, a man in his middle fifties. She
had joined the Bergner firm in 1948, six years after
John Bergner had become the owner of a country house
built in 1865.

Bergner liked to spend his weekends among his favorite employees, and sometimes asked some of the office boys as well as his two secretaries to come up to
Connecticut with him. All was most idyllic until the early
1950s, when John Bergner met an advertising man by
the name of Philip Mervin. This business relationship
soon broadened into a social friendship, and before long
Mr. Mervin was a steady and often self-invited house
guest in Westbrook.

At first, this did not disturb anyone very much, but when Mervin noticed the deep and growing friendship between Bergner and his right-hand girl, something akin to jealousy prompted him to interfere with this relationship at every turn. What made this triangle even more difficult for Mervin to bear was the apparent innocence with which Bergner treated Mervin's approaches. Naturally, a feeling of dislike grew into hatred between Miss Rivers and the intruder, but before it came to any open argument, the advertising man suddenly died of a heart attack at age fifty-one.

But that did not seem to be the end of it by a long shot.

Soon after his demise, the Connecticut weekends were again interrupted, this time by strange noises no natural cause could account for. Most of the uncanny experiences were witnessed by both girls as well as by some of the office boys, who seemed frightened by it all. With the detachment of a good executive secretary, Miss Rivers listed the phenomena:

Objects moving in space.

Stones hurled at us inside and outside the house.

Clanging of tools in the garage at night (when nobody was there).

Washing machine starting up at 1 A.M., *by itself*.

Heavy footsteps, banging of doors, in the middle of the night.

Television sets turning themselves on and off at will.

A spoon constantly leaping out of a cutlery tray.

The feeling of a cold wind being swept over one.

And there was more, much more.

When a priest was brought to the house to exorcise the ghost, things only got worse. Evidently the deceased had little regard for holy men.

Juliet, the other secretary, brought her husband along. One night in 1962, when Juliet's husband slept in what was once the advertising man's favorite guest room, he heard clearly a series of knocks, as if someone were hitting the top of the bureau. Needless to say, her husband had been alone in the room, and he did not do the knocking.

It became so bad that Grace Rivers no longer looked forward to those weekend invitations at her employer's country home. She feared them. It was then that she remembered, with terrifying suddenness, a remark the late Mr. Mervin had made to her fellow workers.

"If anything ever happens to me and I die, I'm going to walk after those two girls the rest of their lives!" he had said.

Miss Rivers realized that he was keeping his word.

Her only hope was that the ghost of Mr. Mervin would someday be distracted by an earlier specter that was sharing the house with him. On several occasions, an old woman in black had been seen emerging from a side door of the house. A local man, sitting in front of the house during the weekdays when it was unoccupied (Bergner came up only on weekends) was wondering aloud to Miss Rivers about the "old lady who claimed she occupied the back part of the house." He had encountered her on many occasions, always seeing her disappear into the house by that same, seldom-used side door. One of the office boys invited by John Bergner also saw her around 1:30 A.M. on a Sunday morning, when he stood outside the house, unable to sleep. When she saw him she said hello, mentioned something about money, then disappeared into a field.

Grace Rivers looked into the background of the house and discovered that it had previously belonged to a very aged man who lived there with his mother. When she died, he found money buried in the house, but he claimed his mother had hidden more money that he had never been able to locate. Evidently the ghost of his mother felt the same way about it, and was still searching. For that's how it is with ghosts sometimes—they become forgetful about material things.

Finally, romance beyond the grave can also involve a jealous lover who resents the "replacement" taking his or her place in the affections of the former mate still enjoying the physical life in all its glory. Such was the case with Sylvia W., who never thought a *menage à trois* could—or should—involve a ghost!

Sylvia W. is in her late twenties, has been married twice and has lived a full and normally exciting life. Since the age of eight she has had precognitive experiences, warnings, feelings about impending events—many of which have come true—and psychic dreams. She has always accepted the importance of ESP in her life and never had any fears of the so-called occult. But recently something has happened in her life that has her stumped. She has fallen in love with a widower, Albert, whose wife and infant daughter were killed in a motor-car accident in 1961. Albert's wife herself had had a premonition of the impending accident and had told him so. Moreover, three days after her death she appeared before him and assured him that she would always be with him and take care of him. Before her passing she had earnestly requested that should she die he should not remarry. He did not promise this.

As soon as Albert had gotten over the shock of his wife's untimely passing he began to mingle socially once again. He and Sylvia had originally met because her house was rented from his company, and they became involved with each other in a love relationship. They dated for about six months, and the first four months of their relationship were undisturbed and harmonious. But then unusual things started to happen. Strange noises and movements occurred both in her house and in his. That was not surprising since they spent time in both. There were knockings on the door (mainly late at night) but when they opened it no one was there. Then there were sounds of someone walking in the next room or heavy objects seemingly dropping to the floor. Upon investigation they found nothing to substantiate the noises. On occasion the blinds would open by themselves or a book would move of its own volition and open to a certain page while the room in which this happened was closed off and no one had access to it. Apparently someone was trying to convey messages to Albert, for the books were marked at different passages. When they read one of the passages in a particular novel that had been left in a conspicuous spot, they realized who was behind the phenomena. The passage in the book dealt with a female competitor who was domineering, about honest love, and about one partner being "from another world." And one passage referred to someone having seen the light.

Fantastic as it seemed at first, they realized that the dead wife was trying from the beyond to break up their romance. When they were together during the night there was a knocking on the window. Albert got up to investigate outside. After he had left the bedroom Sylvia rose and looked out onto the patio through the blinds. The lights were on in the patio and she assumed that Albert was checking that area of the house. Also, she clearly heard the door to the kitchen open and close and lock itself. After Albert returned she learned that he had not even been in the back of the house where the patio and kitchen are located. He had been to the front only. In the middle of the night they tried to go over the phenomena and make some sense out of them. In listing them they realized that the disturbances had started just about the time Albert had declared his love for Sylvia. Moreover, Sylvia had just borrowed an object that had belonged to Albert's first wife. It was a typewriter. She had left it on the floor only to find it moved the following morning back to the shelf where it had originally been. No one had been near it during the night. That is to say, no one of flesh and blood. What were they to do? Pending a visit to me I explained that they must address the deceased woman and explain the facts of life to her or perhaps the facts of "after life." Only by making her understand the error of her ways could they hope to release her from her compulsion and themselves from her interference. I have not heard from Sylvia since then and can only hope that it worked.

LOVE AND CARE BEYOND THE GRAVE

iane Schmitt was a level-headed twenty-one-year-old. Until age seventeen, she had not shown the slightest interest in psychic matters. She lived with her parents in a medium-sized town in Michigan. Her friend Kerm was the apple of her eye, and vice versa. No doubt, if things had proceeded normally, they would have married.

But one night after he had driven her home, Kerm was killed in a car accident on the way to his own place. The shock hit Diane very strongly, and she missed him. She wondered whether there was anything in the belief that man survived death.

One week after the funeral of her friend, she smelled the scent of funeral flowers on arising. For five days, this phenomenon took place. There were no such flowers in the house at the time. Then other things followed. Diane was on her way home from a girlfriend's house around midnight. As she drove home, she gradually felt another presence with her in the car. She laughed it off as being due to an overactive imagination, but the sensation persisted. She looked around for a moment, but the back seat was empty. Again she focused her eyes on the road. Suddenly she felt something touch first her left hand, then her right. There was no mistaking it; the touch was very real.

At another time she awoke in the middle of a sound sleep. She felt the presence of something or someone in the room with her. Finally, she opened her eyes and looked in all directions. She saw nothing unusual, but she was sure there was another person sitting on the second bed, watching her. The feeling became so intense that she broke out in a cold sweat. But she did not dare get up, and finally she managed to get back to sleep. The next morning, when she awoke, her first act was to have a look at the other bed. There, at the foot of the bed, was an imprint on the bedspread, as if someone had been sitting on it!

After that there was a period of quiet, and Diane thought with great relief that the psychic manifestations had finally come to an end.

But in late July 1965, something happened that caused her to reconsider that opinion. A young man named Jerry had been a steady companion of hers since the unfortunate accident in which Kerm had been killed. There was a party at Diane's house one evening. After company had left, Jerry stayed on.

Together they sat and talked for several hours. It grew late and dawn began to show itself. The two young people were sitting on the couch downstairs when suddenly Jerry looked up and asked if her mother was standing at the top of the stairs! Diane knew that her mother would be asleep in her room, yet she followed Jerry's eyes to the top landing of the stairs.

There was a figure standing there, rather vaguely outlined and seemingly composed of a white filmy substance. At its base there was a luminous sparkle. As the two young people stared at the figure, without daring to move, it gradually faded away.

Jerry then left for home and Diane went to bed. As he drove down the road, he was about to pass the spot where Kerm had been killed a few months before. He stopped for a moment and got out to stretch his legs. When he walked back to his car, he noticed that it was enveloped by a thick fog. He got into the car, which felt strangely cold and clammy. He glanced to his right, and to his horror he saw a white, cloudlike object cross the road toward the car. As it approached the car, Jerry could make it out clearly enough: it was a blurred image of a human body, but the face was as plain as day. It was Kerm. He got into the front seat with Jerry, who shook with terror. His eyes were watering and he dared not move.

"Take care of Di," a strangely broken voice said next to him. It sounded as though it were coming from far away, like an echo.

Then a hand reached out for his and Jerry passed out. When he came to, he found himself parked in front of the local cemetery. How he had got there he did not know. It was some distance from the spot of Kerm's accident to the cemetery. But there he was, barely able to start his car and drive home.

When he told his story to his parents, they thought he had dreamed it. Jerry was sure he had not. The events that followed bore him out. It would seem that Kerm wanted to make sure Jerry took good care of his former girlfriend. At various times, Jerry would feel a hand at his shoulder.

At this point Diane got in touch with me. As I could not then rush out to Michigan, I sent her explicit instructions about what to do. On the next occasion when the restless form was in evidence, she was to address him calmly and ask that he cease worrying over her. Jerry would indeed look out for her, and they would rather not have him, Kerm, around also. Three does make a crowd, even if one is a ghost.

Apparently Kerm took the hint and left for good. But to Diane it is an indication that there is another world where we all may meet again.

Miss Sally S. lived in what was then a nice section of Brooklyn, half an hour from Manhattan and, at the time of the happenings I am about to report, was semiretired, working two days a week at her old trade of being a secretary. A year after the first phenomena occurred, she moved away to Long Island, not because of her ghostly experiences, but because the neighborhood had become too noisy for her: ghosts she could stand, human disturbances were too much.

Miss S. moved into her Brooklyn apartment in May of the same year. At first, it seemed nice and quiet. Then, on August 3, she had an unusual experience. It must have been around three A.M. when she awoke with an uncanny feeling that there was an intruder in her place. She looked out into the room, and in the semi-darkness saw what appeared to be a dark figure. It was a man, and though she could not make out any features, he seemed tall and as lifelike as any human intruder might be.

Thinking that it was best for her to play possum,

she lay still and waited for the intruder to leave. Picture her shock and surprise when the figure approached her and started to touch her quilt cover. About fifteen minutes prior to this experience, she had awakened because she was cold, and had pulled the cover over herself. Thus she was very much awake when the "intruder" appeared to her. She lay still, trembling, watching his every move. Suddenly he vanished into thin air, and it was only then that Miss S. realized she wasn't dealing with any flesh-and-blood person, but a ghost.

A month later, again around three A.M., Miss S. awoke to see a white figure gliding back and forth in her room. This time, however, she was somewhat sleepy, so she did not feel like doing much about it. However, when the figure came close to her bed, she stuck out her arm to touch it, and at that moment it dissolved into thin air. Wondering who the ghost might be, Miss S. had another opportunity to observe it in November, when around six A.M. she went into her kitchen to see the dark outline of a six-foot-tall man standing in the archway between the kitchen and dinette. She looked away for a moment, and then returned her gaze to the spot. The apparition was still there. Once more Miss S. closed her eyes and looked away, and when she returned her eyes to the spot, he was gone.

She decided to speak to her landlady about the incidents. The owner of the house assured her that no one had died in the house, nor had there been any tragedy, to the best of her knowledge. As for a previous owner, she wouldn't know. Miss S. realized that it was her peculiar psychic talent that made the phenomena possible. For some time now she had been able to predict the results of horse races with uncanny accuracy, getting somewhat of a reputation in the area. Even during her school days, she came up with answers she had not yet been taught. In April of the next year, Miss S. visited her sister and her husband in New Jersey. They had bought a house the year before, and knew nothing of its history. Sally was assigned a finished room in the attic. Shortly after two A.M., a ghost appeared to her in that room. But before she could make out any details, the figure vanished. By now Miss S. knew that she had a talent for such things, and preferred not to talk about them with her sister, a somewhat nervous individual. But she kept wondering who the ghost at *her* house was.

Fourteen years earlier, a close friend named John had passed away. A year before, he had given her two nice fountain pens as gifts, and Miss S. had kept one at home, and used the other at her office. A year after her friend's death, she was using one of the pens in the office when the point broke. Because she couldn't use it anymore, she put the pen into her desk drawer. Then she left the office for a few minutes. When she returned, she found a lovely, streamlined black pen on top of her desk. She immediately inquired whether any of the girls had left it there, but no one had, nor had anyone been near her desk. The pen was a rather expensive Mont Blanc, just the thing she needed. It made her wonder whether her late friend John had not presented her with it even from the Beyond.

This belief was reinforced by an experience she had had on the first anniversary of his passing, when she heard his voice loud and clear calling her "sweetheart" —the name he had always used to address her, rather than her given name, Sally.

All this ran through her head fourteen years later,

when she tried to come to terms with her ghostly experiences. Was the ghost someone who came with the house, someone who had been there before, or was it someone who somehow linked up with her? Then Sally began to put two and two together. She was in the habit of leaving her feet outside her quilt cover because the room was rather warm with the heat on. However, in the course of the night, the temperature in the room fell, and frequently her feet became almost frostbitten as a result. One Saturday night in March, the same year she visited her sister, she was still awake, lying in bed around eleven P.M. Her feet were sticking out of the quilt, as the temperature was still tolerable. Suddenly she felt a terrific tug on her quilt; it was first raised from above her ankles, and then pulled down to cover her feet. Yet she saw no one actually doing it.

Suddenly she remembered how her late friend John had covered her feet when she had fallen asleep after one of his visits with her. Evidently he was still concerned that Sally should not get cold feet, or worse, and had decided to watch over her in this manner.

When the object of one man's love might also be coveted by another man, and death has come between them, one of the men might develop an ongoing need to "stay in touch," partly because his feelings continue beyond an untimely death, and partly because of the "other man." Roseanne Schaffer is a very attractive, self-assured young woman of thirty-six who makes her living in several ways. She has a regular part as an Oriental dancer on one of the soap operas, and does Eastern dancing under the name Fahrushka, which means butterfly. She is also a very busy tarot reader and psychic consultant, appearing all over the country at fairs, colleges, and clubs. Since her father was psychic, the subject was never disbelieved at home; her father was a marine engineer and mediums, psychics, and séances were always part of their lives in Union City, New Jersey.

When Roseanne was only a precocious (but very attractive) fourteen, she caught the eye of two young men several years older than herself. One of the boys, Vincent, eighteen, joined the Navy but was brutally murdered three years later. The other young man, Dennis, also died violently shortly after. She and Dennis met at a masonic convention when Dennis was eighteen, and the bond was there instantly. They dated for several years, even though a physical relationship did not develop due to her young age.

When she was in a school play, Dennis came to a rehearsal to see her. But when she saw his silhouette entering the auditorium, something very strange occurred. Roseanne suddenly felt herself transported back in time, wearing old-fashioned clothes and having the appearance of a woman of about twenty-four to twenty-eight. A young man of about thirty or so came down what appeared to be a walkway in New England, and they met and embraced with a feeling of incredible joy. Twenty seconds later, she was "back" in real time, still fifteen years old, and the stranger was just Dennis. But had this been a flashback to an earlier lifetime she and Dennis had shared?

Dennis worked as a breakman for the railroad. One day there was a terrible accident: Dennis was crushed between cars and died at the hospital shortly after. At the time Roseanne had not seen him for several months, and only saw his obituary later. By now she was in col-

lege and was dating another man. At the time Dennis
died, in November 1973, she had been eighteen and he
twenty-two.

Shortly after she had become aware of the deaths of
both these young men, she experienced a strange sensation in the early mornings. It felt like a "waking dream"
in which she could not wake up even though she was
fully aware of that fact and her surroundings. Then
there was a tingling sensation all over her face and neck,
as if she was being touched by something electric. It
dawned on her that "someone" was trying to get in
touch with her—but which one of the two young men
who had died so tragically at almost the same time? She
was soon to know. The dreams came more often now,
and it was always she and Dennis enjoying each other's
company—and yet she heard herself say in the dreams,
"But you are dead!" Once or twice she heard her name
called softly, just "Rose . . ." and the tingling of her
face and neck indeed felt like kisses . . . kisses from the
Beyond. Roseanne is not upset by all this, even though
Dennis is still "hanging around."

When a couple has been together a long time and
has really cared for one another, it may be difficult for
the surviving partner to accept the separation, even if it
is relatively temporary. But sometimes it is also unacceptable to the one who has died and now finds himself
very much "alive," contrary to what he has been told all
his life about what happens to us at "death." So, naturally, it is only a short step to wanting to continue the
old relationship. In some cases, which I will report further on, this can even become a physical contact. In others, it is a spiritual bond, and communication occurs
either directly or through a medium. A particular case I

recently heard about is more bizarre than anything I have investigated until now, and is certainly not recommended as a proper way to continue a relationship "beyond the grave."

A German magazine recently reported how the widow of a prominent businessman continued her rather active sex life with him even after his demise. Mrs. B. kept receiving concrete directives from her late husband, ordering her to invite likely candidates to her home so that the late husband could possess their bodies and thus satisfy his cravings through the intermediary of other people's physical bodies. Apparently the attempt to continue their active sexual relationship from the beyond wasn't altogether successful. Mrs. B. continued to look. In the course of her search for likely candidates to lend her discarnate husband a temporary body, dozens upon dozens of likely young men populated her bed. To the relatives, such behavior was, of course, unspeakable, especially since a rich inheritance was involved. But to Mrs. B. it seemed perfectly natural that her husband would want to continue their thirty years of happy relationship without benefit of a physical body, if he was able to swing it. And swing it he did. Apparently Mr. B.'s sexual appetites became more sophisticated as time went on. No longer satisfied with simple intercourse with his wife, he craved group sex as well, keeping up with the trends of the times. Since Mrs. B. did not possess any contacts with people willing to perform such unusual actions on behalf of her late husband, she used the classified ads in a German newspaper to find likely candidates. As far as the "candidates" were concerned, so long as they got paid well, it did not matter whether they were addressed by another man's name during intercourse.

Word of the strange goings-on in Mrs. B.'s house could not fail to reach wider circles and Mrs. B.'s reputation became such that her old friends stayed away from her. However, no one could accuse her of improper acts. She was neither insane nor did she break the law in any way. Thus Mrs. B. was able to continue her enjoyment of life as she saw it, or rather as the voice of her late husband speaking to her from beyond would want it. Apparently Mr. B. did not lack a somewhat unusual sense of humor. He directed his wife to arrange to have someone with her in the cemetery in order to make love on his grave. He promised to be there and make the occasion worthwhile. Only the purely technical aspects of arranging such a get-together in a cemetery have kept Mrs. B. so far from realizing thus far her husband's latest desire.

LOVE LOST, AND FOUND, BEYOND THE CENTURIES

When a romantic relationship is thwarted or suddenly disrupted and both parties pass on with love unfullfilled, it sometimes happens that they reach out to one another over the centuries and try to connect again, perhaps even resume what was not possible before. Such situations involve reincarnation, of course, but more than that they may entail an enduring search for the other person over much time, perhaps even several incarnations, to set things right in the end.

Catharine Warren-Browne was born in Lancashire, England, daughter of a naval commander who was killed at sea in 1939 as a result of the Second World War. She is descended from an old Northumbrian family on her mother's side, and many of her paternal ancestors were naval officers, including Admiral Blake. Her family is highly respected in England; many of her ancestors have sat in Parliament, and some are noblemen.

Catharine led an interesting and unusual life while

in England. On many occasions she had psychic experiences, ranging from knowledge of future events to the ability to see ghosts and experience the uncanny in houses in which her family lived or where she was visiting; but her psychic experiences do not properly belong here, astounding though they may be. She had visions of events in the past, experiences with displacements in time that too were truly amazing.

The family is Catholic, and she comes from an area of England that is even today predominantly Catholic. Many of her friends have been priests or abbots, and she considers herself a very good Catholic to this day, even though she wonders why the Church does not pay greater attention to the reality of psychic phenomena. She knows only too well that these things are happening and that they are by no means evil or to be feared.

She and her husband had been living in an old priory in 1959 when his father died and left them to cope with estate taxes. English inheritance taxes are staggering; thus, the money left them by Mr. Warren-Browne's father was taxed to the tune of 92 percent. Under these circumstances they found it impossible to carry on life in England. They had to sell the house and farm, and in 1959 they came to America to start life all over at the ages of thirty-eight and forty-two.

When I met the Warren-Brownes in Hollywood in 1968, I found them to be friendly, unassuming people. Mr. Warren-Browne was most interested in his new program of boat-building, a career he had recently started, while Mrs. Warren-Browne was particularly keen on doing a novel about a period that she found herself strangely involved in—sixteenth-century England. As a result of our conversations, I later went to England to follow up on some of the things that had happened to Catharine in her earlier years.

She has always found great comfort in her Roman Catholic religion, and when she moved to an old priory of the Knights Templars near Ross-on-Wye, she reopened the chapel with permission of the Church and had priests from nearby Belmont Abbey say mass there now and again. As a consequence, she received an authentic reliquary from Monsignor Montini, who later became pope. Although she had occasionally discussed the question of reincarnation with her monastic friends, it wasn't of particular interest to her one way or the other.

Now in retrospect certain incidents make sense to her, although at the time they seemed to be completely out of context and truly strange. When Catharine was only thirteen years old, the family had a governess by the name of Miss Gant. Catharine's mother liked her very much because Miss Gant was very learned. The children did not like her because they found her to be a fanatic and given to holding forth on various subjects in history at the breakfast table. On one such occasion the conversation turned to the life of Henry VIII. A book about this king had just been published, and Miss Gant remarked that he had just been a monster, worse than Caligula. At this, Catharine became suddenly very agitated and remarked that she was wrong. "Henry was a misunderstood man," she said quietly. Her mother insisted that she apologize to the governess, but ignoring her own mother, Catharine went on to speak of the life of Henry VIII as if she had known him intimately.

"The subject is closed," Miss Gant said rather snidely. "He was a very unpleasant man, and God punished him. He died of a very horrible disease." But Catharine's father backed her up at this point and let her have her say. In quasi-medical terms young Catharine now described Henry VIII's fatal illness, denying that he had ever had syphilis and in the process shocking her mother, and remarking that the king had died of obesity and a varicose ulcer in his leg that would not heal due to a high blood-sugar content. Such knowledge on the part of a thirteen-year-old girl was amazing, but even Catharine thought no more of it at the time. There may have been other incidents bearing on the matter at hand but Catharine does not recall them.

In 1957 she was very ill, recuperating at a private hospital in Bath, England. Due to a fall, she had had some surgery and was on the critical list when a close friend, the Abbot Alphege Gleason, came to visit her at the hospital. He stepped up to her bed and said, "Poor Catharine, what are they doing to you?" Very sleepily, the patient replied, "Here is good Master Coverdale come to comfort me." Her visitor was taken aback. "Master Coverdale?" he said. "You are a learned young woman, but I should have thought I might have been taken for Cranmer, whom I'd always admired," he replied with a smile. By now Catharine was fully awake and asked, "Who on earth is Coverdale?" Many years later she discovered that Dr. Coverdale was a preacher friend and protégé of Katharine Parr, one of the queens of Henry VIII.

Mrs. Warren-Browne has had eight pregnancies but, due to a blood factor, has only three living children. On several occasions she would be in good spirits right up to the impending birth. At that point she would break into uncontrollable tears for no apparent reason.

On one occasion, she was asked by her physician, Dr. Farr, in Sussex, England, why she felt so depressed at this particular point when all seemed to be going so well. For no apparent reason Mrs. Warren-Browne replied, "She was healthy, too, but she died of puerperal fever." The doctor asked whom she was talking about, and Mrs. Warren-Browne truthfully replied she did not know, nor did she have any idea why she had made the remark. The doctor then proceeded to tell her that this disease no longer presented any threat to mothers because it had been brought under control through modern methods, but that it was indeed a fatal disease centuries ago. Years later, research established that Katharine Parr did indeed die of that disease.

After Mrs. Warren-Browne's son Giles was born, she became very ill and had what she called waking dreams, in the sense that they were far more realistic than ordinary dreams are. Suddenly, she saw herself as a woman almost dead in a great canopied bed. The woman had long, red-gold hair. Then Mrs. Warren-Browne would come out of this state and feel very depressed and sorry for the woman she had seen in her vision, but she always shrugged it off as a rather fanciful dream.

Ten years went by, and if there were incidents relating to the period of Henry VIII, they escaped Mrs. Warren-Browne's attention in the course of her daily activities. She has a good education, and her knowledge of history now is equal to that of anyone with her background, but she has never had any particular interest in the period of Henry VIII other than what any Englishwoman might have. As for Katharine Parr, the name meant little to her except that she recalled it from her school days as the name of one of the wives of Henry VIII. Beyond that, there seemed to be no conscious connection.

In September of 1968 she and her husband happened to be in Iowa. He had some business there, and she was working on a book off and on as time permitted. She owned a pack of alphabet cards, and as she went about her work, she kept finding these cards arranged to spell the word Parr. She had not done this, nor was anyone around who could have so arranged the cards. She recognized the name Parr and thought that perhaps it had something to do with an ancestor of her family's on her mother's side. For, a long time back, there had been some connection with the Parr family of Northumberland.

Since she had no one to discuss this with, she decided to try the method of divining by pendulum. She put her wedding ring on a thread, and to her amazement it worked. There was indeed someone present who wished to communicate with her, and being fully aware of her psychic past, she did not reject this notion out of hand. Instead she decided it would be more practical to have an alphabet to work with, so she got out her Ouija board, and despite her feelings that such a board represented mainly a person's unconscious mind, she decided to give it a try.

"Who is there?" she asked.

Immediately the board gave her an answer. "Seymour," it spelled.

"Are you my Uncle Seymour?" she asked, for she could think of no relative other than her uncle who might want to communicate with her.

"No," the communicator said sternly, "Tom Seymour."

It still didn't ring any bells in her mind. "Which Tom Seymour?" she asked.

There was a pause. Then the entity operating through the board replied, "The Lord Admiral."

This gave Catharine pause for thought, and then she decided to investigate this communicator more closely.

"When were you born?"

"Fifteen-o-three."

"Why do you want to get in touch with me?"

"Long have I waited," the board spelled out.

"What have you waited for?" Catharine asked.

The whole thing became more and more ludicrous to her. Her suspicious mind was ready to blame her subconscious self for all this nonsense, or so she thought. She knew enough about extrasensory perception to realize that there were also pitfalls that a sensible individual had to avoid. She wasn't about to fall into such a trap.

"For you, Kate." Now, no one has ever called Catharine Warren-Browne Kate except her father, so she was rather dubious about the genuineness of the conversation.

Immediately, she thought of what she had read that could have some bearing on all this. Years before, she had read *The Wives of Henry VIII*, but that had been in her school days. More to amuse herself than because she accepted the communication as genuine, she continued working the Ouija board.

The unknown communicator insisted that he was Tom Seymour, and that she, Catharine Warren-Browne, was Katharine Parr reincarnated. The notion struck Mrs. Warren-Browne as preposterous. She knew, of course, that Katharine Parr was the last wife of Henry VIII, the only one who managed him well and who survived him, but she had never heard of Tom Seymour. It is well to state here that all her research in this came after most of the information had come to her either through the Ouija board or in dream/visions.

Today, of course, she has a fairly good knowledge of the period, having even decided to write a romantic novel about it, but at the time of the initial communications in 1968, she knew no more about Henry VIII and his queens than any well-educated Englishwoman would know.

The communicator who had identified himself as Tom Seymour advised her among other things that she was buried at Sudely. Now, Mrs. Warren-Browne had always assumed that Queen Katharine Parr was buried in the royal burial vault at Windsor, but upon checking this out, she found to her amazement that Katharine Parr had indeed been laid to rest at Sudely, an old castle at the border of Worcestershire and Herefordshire.

Later she was able to find references to Tom Seymour in historical records. She learned that Tom Seymour and the widowed Queen Katharine had married after the death of King Henry VIII. Their marriage had lasted about eighteen months, until she died in childbirth. Tom had survived her by about a year, when he was executed for political intrigue.

At the time of the first communications through the Ouija board, Mrs. Warren-Browne did not know this, nor did she know the name of the child, the only child "she" and Tom Seymour had had. Tom referred to the child as Mary. Mrs. Warren-Browne very much doubted this, assuming that the child would have been called Jane, since Jane Seymour was Tom's sister and a close friend of Katharine Parr; however, research proved the communicator right. The child's name was Mary.

All during October of 1968 she felt herself drawn to the Ouija board and compelled to write down as quickly as she could whatever was given her by that means. She didn't want to believe the authenticity of that material, and yet she felt that in view of her earlier psychic experiences, she should at least have someone look into this and authenticate the whole matter if possible, or reject it if that were to be the case.

Thus in December of 1968 she contacted me. When we met the following spring, we went over all the communications she had had until that time. "What indication do you have that you are Katharine Parr reincarnated?" I began.

"Well, this is what *he* thinks," Mrs. Warren-Browne replied politely, "unless, of course, it is something from the subconscious mind."

"What are Tom Seymour's reasons to assume you are his long-lost Katharine?"

"Well, he keeps saying that he's tried to reach me for years, that he's been waiting and waiting, and I replied, 'Katharine Parr is dead. Why are you not together now?' "

"And how does he explain that?" I asked.

"They are on different planes, on different levels," she explained.

"But you were reborn because you were in a more advanced state."

The communications between Mrs. Warren-

Browne and Tom Seymour went on for about a month. There was still some doubt in Mrs. Warren-Browne's mind as to the authenticity of the whole thing. On one occasion, the communicator referred to the date on which their child had been born. Tom had insisted that it was August 17. Mrs. Warren-Browne looked it up at the library and found that the child had been born on August 28 and died eight days later. The next evening she reminded her communicator he had made a mistake in his calculation. "No," Tom Seymour replied through the board. "We had the Julian calendar, you have the Gregorian calendar." Quickly she checked this and found that he was right. The difference of eleven days was accounted for by the difference of the calendars.

"Before this communication came, did you ever have any slips in time when you felt you were someone else?" I asked Mrs. Warren-Browne.

"Not that I have felt I'm someone else but that I have known places that I have been to."

"For instance?"

"Pembroke Castle. When my uncle took me there, I said to him, 'Now we are going to such and such a room, which was where Henry the Seventh was born, who was Henry the Eighth's father.' "

"And how did your uncle react to this information?"

"Well, he was of course surprised, but you see, if I had indeed been Katharine Parr, I would have known this because Henry the Seventh was her father-in-law."

"Is there anything else that reminds you of the fifteenth or sixteenth century?" I asked.

"Yes, many times I will catch myself saying something that sounds unfamiliar in today's use and yet that fits perfectly with the earlier period in English history."

"Any strange dreams?"

"Yes, but of course I would consider them just wishful thinking. Sometimes I would see myself wearing long gorgeous dresses, and it seemed that I was someone else."

I suggested we try a regression experiment, but since Mrs. Warren-Browne's husband was present and both were somewhat pressed for time, I felt that this was not the best moment to try it. We said good-by for the moment, and I promised myself to take the first possible opportunity to regress Mrs. Warren-Browne back into the period in which she thought she might have lived. There wasn't sufficient time the following day to call her back to try my hand at regressing her then. Also, they lived quite a distance away, and it seemed impossible to ask them to drive all the way to Hollywood again. But my time schedule was suddenly and unexpectedly rearranged. An appointment I had made for the following morning was canceled, and so I felt almost compelled to pick up the telephone and call Mrs. Warren-Browne. I explained that I had some free time after all and would it be possible for her to come back again so that we could attempt our first regression session. She readily agreed and within a matter of hours she arrived in Hollywood. I then proceeded in the usual way to put her into deep hypnosis. It did not take overly long, for Mrs. Warren-Browne, being mediumistic, was already attuned to this process.

I first took her back into her own childhood, making sure that the transition to another lifetime was gradual. She had come alone this time, perhaps because the presence of her husband might, in her own mind, impede her ability to relax completely, something very necessary for a successful regression.

When I had taken her back to her childhood, she spoke in great detail of her home in England and the staff they had. I then proceeded to send her back even farther, and we were on our way to finding Katharine Parr.

"You're going backward into the past before your birth; way back, until you can find you're someone else. What do you see?"

"I see a home with stone . . . it's Sudely."

"Whom does it belong to?"

"Belongs to Admiral Seymour . . ."

"Do you see yourself?"

"Yes, I see myself."

"Who are you?"

"*He* calls me Kate. I'm terribly cold. I called the doctor, told him how cold it is. Dr. Tahilcus, he was so good."

"Are you ill?"

"Yes."

"What do you have?"

"A fever."

"Is anyone else with you?"

"Dr. Herk. He is the king's physician."

"Who else?"

"My sister, Anne, and Herbert, and Lucy Tibbett, my stepdaughter. Lucy was a poor girl. She didn't like me when I married her father at first. Then she grew very fond of me. Lucy was most faithful. Lucy and Anne kept our marriage secret. I'm so cold, cold, cold."

"How old are you now?"

"Thirty-six."

"I want you to look back now, see what happens to you. You recover from this illness?"

"No, No."

"What happens to you?"

"I go away. I die. I die. I knew it would happen."

"Where do you die?"

"At Sudely."

"What happens to you immediately after you die?"

"Tom is upset, he goes, I'm buried."

"Where are you buried?"

"At Sudely."

"In what part?"

"In the chapel beneath the altar."

"What is on the stone?"

"HERE LIES . . . HERE LIES KATHARINE— THE QUEEN DOWAGER—BARONESS SEYMOUR SUDELY—Kate Parr—Katharine . . . Katharine the Queen. I never wanted that irony."

"Who is buried next to you?"

"No one, no one. He was gone. He was gone, and I loved him and I was angry with him. The Protector told me he was seducing young Bess. I believed it for a time."

"Who was young Bess?"

"The king's daughter."

"Who seduced her?"

"The Protector said that Tom did."

"What is his name?"

"Edward Seymour, Tom's brother. Edward Seymour hated Tom. He hated Tom's popularity. He hated the king's love for him. He was scheming. They even denied me my dowager rights. I had several manors and

I had dowries from my two husbands before—Lord Latimer, John Neville—good men."

"I want you to look at the chapel now. What is next to your tombstone?"

"Next to my stone . . . It's beneath the altar, a wall, and it fell. It fell on Cromwell's men. Cromwell's men desecrated my tomb."

"Is it still there?"

"It was rebuilt in later centuries."

"Can you see the windows of the chapel?"

"It was an oriel window, but it's changed. I left because Tom is not there. They took his body."

"Where did they put it?"

"They took his body back to Wiltshire. His family took it. Tom came from Wilkes Hall, in Wiltshire."

"Is he still there?"

"I don't know. I haven't found him since."

"Do you see him now?"

"I remember him. He had black hair, dark blue eyes; he was always tanned. He was at sea a lot. His brother was a cold fish."

"When you died, what did you do immediately afterwards?"

"I remember looking at him. He was sad, and I was sorry that I had not trusted him."

"Did you see your body?"

"Oh, yes, just *as a shell*."

"Where were you?"

"In my bedroom in Sudely. My spirit got up. My body was taken."

"What did your spirit look like?"

"How does a spirit look?"

"Did you wear clothes?"

"I suppose so. I suppose so, but they couldn't see me."

"Where did you go then?"

"I went to Hampton."

"Why?"

"That's were we had been so happy. I went to Hampton because Tom had liked it. He couldn't bear Sudely."

"Where is Hampton?"

"Hampton Court, and his house in Chelsea."

"Did anyone see you?"

"I don't know."

"What did you do there?"

"I looked around from room to room, but he'd gone. He went north to my home."

"What did you do then?"

"I went to Kendal."

"Where's that?"

"In Westmorland."

"What did you do there?"

"I looked around where I was born. And Tom *went* there. He went up there."

"Did you find him *there?*"

"I saw him but *he* couldn't see *me.*"

"Did you make any attempt to let him know you were there?"

"Oh, yes."

"What did you do?"

"Yes, I put my arms around him, and he shivered. He was sad, and he went to my cousin's. He went to Strickland."

"Where are they located?"

"On the borders near Westmorland."

"And you followed him there?"

"I followed. Then he went away. He had to go into hiding."

"Why?"

"His brother accused him of treason."

"What had he done?"

"Nothing. He had the affection of his nephew, the little king. He had never done anything. His brother accused him of trying to wed with Bess, which wasn't true. Bess was only fifteen. He just used to romp with her. He had no children, just one baby that I left."

"And his brother, Seymour, whose side was he on?"

"He was the Lord Protector, but the little king didn't like him. They kept him short of money, and Tom used to take a little money and give it [to him]. That's why the Lord Protector took the great seal to stamp the documents. He took it away from the king."

"Who did the Lord Protector favor for the crown?"

"Jane Seymour and his son. Not James Seymour. James Seymour was his brother . . . the king's brother. Jane, Jane, she was Jane."

"And what happened?"

"Jane Grey, Lady Jane, she was only a child. She was married to Guildford. He wanted to control the children."

"But how was the Lord Protector related to Jane Grey?"

"I think he was her uncle."

"Then Jane Grey had the right of succession?"

"Rather distantly, but she thought she was a niece of the late King Henry."

"And he favored her cause?"

"Yes, because he knew that little Edward would not live. He had the lung tisk."

"And he then helped Lady Jane to become Queen?"

"Yes, but it only lasted a few days. The poor child. They beheaded just a child."

"What happened to the Protector?"

"He was beheaded too when Mary came. Mary had her good points. Mary had grown sour, but she was a good woman."

"Did she marry?"

"Yes, she was a sad woman. If she'd married younger and been in love younger, she would have been a happier woman, but the Protector tried to kill Mary, and somebody counseled her to hide. Sawston, she hid at Sawston."

"What happened at Sawston?"

"They burned it."

"Yes, and what did she say after it was burned?"

"She said she would reward them and build them better. She was fond of them."

"Do you remember the name of the people that owned Sawston?"

"Huddleston."

"Were they Protestant or Catholic?"

"They were Catholic. The Huddlestons always were . . . I knew a Huddleston in another life."

"You knew a Huddleston?"

"He was a Benedictine priest."

"What was his first name?"

"Gilbert, and in religion it was Roger."

"Tell me this—after you left, after you couldn't find Tom, where did you go?"

"I wandered."

"Did you know you were dead?"

"Yes."

"Did it bother you?"

"I was sad to leave, sometimes content. I was happy in a sense but sad to leave, because somehow we couldn't find each other."

"Were you aware of the passage of time?"

"Not particularly. It seems I was aware of people coming, people changing. People came where I was."

"Where were you most of the time?"

"I don't know how to describe it. It was light. I think it was happiness, but it was not complete happiness."

"Was it a place?"

"It was not just one place. It was . . . it was space, but I could go on the earth."

"How did you do that?"

"I could just will myself. Just will, that's all."

"Now, this place you were in up above the earth, could you look down from it?"

"Yes."

"What did you see?"

"Just a great amount of people, people, places."

"And the place you were in off the earth, did you see people?"

"Oh, yes."

"Did you recognize any of them?"

"My grandmother, my grandmothers."

"Did you speak to them?"

"Yes, you don't speak."

"How did you hear them?"

"We think."

"And the thoughts were immediately understood?"

"Yes, and we could will things for people. We could help sometimes, but not always. Sometimes you would want to prevent something terrible from happening."

"And?"

"So we would try, but not always, you couldn't always. People don't understand."

"Is there some sort of law you had to obey?"

"I don't know. I don't know."

"Was there anyone who took charge? Any authority up there?"

"Yes, in a sense. You felt bound by something, by someone."

"Was it a person?"

"It was a rule."

"Who made the rule?"

"It came from someone higher."

"Did you meet that person?"

"Not really. We saw a great light."

"Above you?"

"Beyond."

"What was the light like?"

"It was clear, bright, bright light."

"Did you speak to the light?"

"Yes."

"How did it answer you?"

"It said to be patient, go on, try to help. I wanted . . . I wanted. I wasn't really unhappy, but I wasn't fully content."

"Did anyone tell you how long you had to stay in this place?"

"No, they said that I could go on farther, or try to help."

"What did you choose?"

"I said I'd try to help, because time doesn't seem very long. Later, when I looked down, I knew the time *was* long."

"Who asked you whether you would want to go on farther? Who?"

"The voice from the light."

"You couldn't see a person?"

"No."

"How did the voice sound?"

"Wonderful."

"Male or female?"

"Male, male."

"Did you question who the voice was?"

"No."

"Did you know who it was?"

"I felt as though it was from God, although not Him in person. I asked, had it asked something."

"What did it tell you?"

"I asked if I had done anything wrong, not to be there where the light was. What was wrong? And he said no, that it was not wrong, that I could choose, that I could choose if I stopped grieving, that I could go ahead, or that I could go back and help."

"If you went ahead, where would you go?"

"To where the light was."

"Did He tell you where that was?"

"Not in words. I just knew that it was ultimate, ultimate peace. I came back and mothered all those children, Henry's children."

"You mothered them?"

"Henry's three children."

"Did any of them ever see you?"

"When?"

"When you were dead."

"Oh, no, but I think that's why I came back."

"When did you come back?"

"I think I had come back so much later. I took care of a lot of children. The war . . . we took care of a lot of children."

"Now, how many years after you had died did you come back?"

"In world years, a long time."

"But you say you took care of children. You mean on earth?"

"Yes, I took care of a lot of Polish children in this last war [World War II]."

"You didn't come back between the time you were up there and the time you're in now?"

"I don't remember. I searched for a long time. I searched for him."

"For Tom? Did you find him?"

"I saw him, but I could never get close."

"He was not up there?"

"Yes, but he wasn't with me, but he seemed to be looking."

"But after his death, did he not join you?"

"Not closely."

"Didn't you ask for him to join you?"

"Yes, I did, I did."

"Why didn't it work?"

"I don't know. He'd look at me; he'd look at me very sadly."

"What did he say?"

"He didn't . . . I don't know."

"Did you ask the light to let you find him?"

"No, I just waited."

"Now, when you came back in your present incarnation, do you remember how you were born? Just before you were born?"

"I remember my mother. She was a beautiful woman."

"When it was time to go down again, did someone tell you when the time had come?"

"I felt it was the time. I seemed to be shown."

"What steps did you take?"

"I didn't take any real steps."

"Was it immediately?"

"No . . . I saw them, but I knew my mother before."

"How did you enter the child's body?"

"I don't think I did by myself. *I was suddenly there.*"

"And what was the first thing you remember?"

"The first thing I remember, they put me to one side because they thought I wouldn't live. They thought I was premature."

"At that moment, did you still remember your previous life?"

"No, it was so dark. There was noise, like I was going through a tunnel, terrible."

"Did you see anything?"

"It was dark and noisy."

"Did you see anything?"

"No, not until after."

"And then what did you see?"

"Then I was in a room. They wrapped me up, but they said I wouldn't live, and I thought, Oh, I have to go back!"

"You remember that?"

"I remember that, and I thought, I must live. I
must live. I had died before, and I was going to be
happy. I was going to. I'd waited so long, eighteen,
twenty years, and then it was so short."

"When you came back, you could actually understand what they were saying?"

"Yes."

"You understood every word?"

"I understood the words. I was premature, and it
was rather difficult."

"And did this knowledge stay with you during the
first few months, or did it disappear again?"

"It went after time. It went until the time when I
was two. When I reached two until I was six, a great
friend from the *other place* used to come and sit by me.
Every night he'd come and sit by me."

"You mean, dead people?"

"Oh, it was wonderful. He came from where the
light was."

"And why did he come?"

"He used to talk to me. He was someone very, very
great."

"Did you remember his name?"

"We didn't call him by name because he was divine."

"Was he your master?"

"He was, yes, you would say 'master.' He sat by my
bed, and then I lost him."

"What do you mean by 'master'?"

"He was what we understood as Christ."

"Is there such a person?"

"Oh, yes."

"Is he the same as the historical Jesus?"

"I think people embellish things, but he is *Christ.*
He is the son of a great spirit."

"Is God a person or is God a principle?"

"Perhaps I'd call it a spirit. I never saw God, but I
knew that one day I would. I would see behind the
light."

"Now, after you came back, had you forgotten these
things?"

"I forgot, but sometimes you dream and remember.
He left when I got older. I realize I was the cause of his
leaving. I was disobedient. It was a childish disobedi-
ence, but he told me that I would find him again, but I
would have to go a long way."

"Did you ever find him again?"

"No, but I will."

"Did you ever find Tom again?"

"I know that I will, because Tom is trying to find
me. Before, he didn't *try* to find me."

"What about Tom? Where is he now?"

"He's waiting to be with me. The time will come."

"Do you think he will pass over again?"

"I think so, this time."

"Why did he have to wait so long?"

"He had things to do."

"What sort of things?"

"He had to wait. He had to *obey* someone."

"What about you?"

"I was widowed at eighteen. I was wed at sixteen to
Lord Borough."

"How old were you when you married Henry?"

"I was thirty-two when I married Lord Latimer. I
was married in St. Paul, Yorkshire. Latimer was a good
man but headstrong."

"Tell me about Henry. What was he like?"

"He was really not as fierce a man as they say."

"How many years were you married to him?"

"He sought my company several times when I was in mourning. He knew me from when Jane was his queen. Jane and I were friends. Jane asked me to take care of her little Edward. Jane died in childbirth fever."

"How did Henry ask you to marry him?"

"He just asked me. He said that he would wed with me. I knew inside that he was going to ask me, and I was hoping that he would ask me to be his mistress, not his wife. I didn't want either, really. I wanted Tom. We felt safer not being married to Henry. A mistress he could pension off. But he didn't have many mistresses, really. He was rather prim."

"How old was he then?"

"He was about fifty-two; he was very, very obese. He was very handsome, virile."

"Now, when you were married, did you celebrate your wedding?"

"Oh, yes."

"What were some of the songs that were sung at your wedding?"

" 'Greensleeves' is one, and a lute song."

"Do you remember the words?"

"I remember some of 'Greensleeves,' not much. Henry wrote music. He wrote one they do not credit him for."

"What was it?"

" 'Western Wind.' "

"How does it go?"

" 'Western wind, when wilt thou blow? With the small rains . . . I caressed my lover in my arms and lie in my bed again.' Henry wrote that, but they missed it. They missed it, I know. Henry played the lute. He was very musical. He was a very clever man. He had a very hot, angry temper, but he was quickly over it. But Gardiner and Wriothesly took advantage of this when they wanted to get rid of someone; they would pick a moment when it was easy to get him angry. That was how he got rid of poor Kate Howard. She was foolish. She was not fit to be queen but he loved her. It was just an old man's love for a girl, and she was vain and silly but she wasn't evil. But they took her away, and they wouldn't let her speak to him. She wanted to speak to him. She knew he would forgive her, put her aside. Henry told me that."

"What had she done?"

"She had committed adultery. She had loved someone else all her life, but she was flattered to marry the king, and you couldn't very well refuse the king's hand. But she should have told him. He begged her to tell him."

"And she didn't do it?"

"No, she was afraid. She was a foolish child."

"And was Henry upset by her death?"

"Yes, he prayed for her. He was angry. He went away. Gardiner and Wriothesly had hastened the execution. Cranmer and Austin. He didn't like the Howards, you see. The Howards were very powerful. He didn't like them, and Henry felt betrayed by them. He had two Howard queens."

"Which was the other one?"

"Anne Boleyn."

"Tell me, why did you pick *this* incarnation, *this*

body, *this* person to speak through? Was there any reason, anything you wanted her to do for you?"

"I was vain. I believe I was considered a good woman, and I loved my husband and I loved Tom. But I had vanity, and I came back into a world which had frightening things. She has tried so many things."

"You mean the woman who has it hard?"

"She's a woman who loves beauty around. She loves beautiful surroundings. It happened at a time when she was young. When she was stupid. She craved for it. This would upset her vanity."

"This is your punishment?"

"Perhaps it is a punishment, but also I wanted to help those children."

I noticed that Mrs. Warren-Browne showed signs of tiring, and as time had passed rather quickly, I decided to bring her back into the present and her incarnation as Mrs. Warren-Browne. This done, she awoke without any recollection of what had transpired in the preceding hour. She felt well and soon was on her way home to rejoin her husband.

All the historical data given by her in the hypnotic state were correct. Some of these are perhaps available in history books, and other data, while available to the specialist in that particular period, are not readily accessible to the average person. Katharine Parr had been twice widowed before she had married Henry VIII. The names of Lord Burgh and Lord Latimer are historical, and her death in childbirth is also factual. After the death of Henry VIII, there was political intrigue in which Tom Seymour fell victim to the machinations of his own brother, the Lord Protector. The fact of Katharine Parr's being buried at Sudely and the account given of the flight of Mary Tudor to escape her political enemies are entirely correct. Mary did hide at Sawston Hall, near Cambridge, which was burned down by her enemies and later rebuilt in great splendor by the queen. Huddleston is indeed the name of the family owning Sawston, and the Huddlestons to this day are a prominent Catholic family. The reference to the entity knowing another Huddleston in this incarnation makes sense if one realizes that Mrs. Warren-Browne was friendly with Father Roger Huddleston in her earlier years in England. Father Huddleston was a Benedictine priest.

But more than the factuality of historical data given, the descriptive passages of life between births and on the other side of life are fascinating and match similar accounts from other sources. It may be difficult for a nonreligious person to accept the visit of the Christ to the young Catharine Warren-Browne, and yet there are other accounts of such visitations. Surely the possibility that the Master looks after his own is not entirely illogical or impossible, for even a nonreligious person will generally grant the historical Jesus his great status as a teacher and healer.

On June 4, 1969, the day after our last meeting, Mrs. Warren-Browne had a meaningful dream, which she proceeded to report to me immediately. The following night she had another dream, also tying in with the regression experiment. Here are her reports.

DREAM #1

I sleep badly, and was awake until after 3:00 A.M., so this took place between 3:00 and 5:00 A.M. It was in color, and voices appeared to be normal or real. We were riding through woodland or heath country, am

sure it was Richmond, the Surrey side of London. I
was still Latimer's wife. Lucy Tyrwhitt, my stepdaughter by Lord Borough, rode with me. We were with the
King's party; he was hawking. There were bearers
and hawk boys, hounds, etc. Tom was there, home
from France; he and Henry wore the Tudor colors of
green and white. I felt very happy; in fact, happiness
permeated the dream. It was a wonderful morning,
early and misty, sun breaking through, the smell of
crushed grass beneath hooves and gorse. I rode a
gray; Tom rode beside me whenever he could, although Henry would keep bellowing for him. They
were on terms of great friendship.

Henry rode an enormous horse, dark bay. He
was very heavy but rode magnificently. We cantered
up a grassy slope to a clearing, and Henry released
his hawk. He removed her hood, undid the leash
from jesses, and threw her. She darted up in circles,
and we all watched. In a very few minutes, she had
sighted her quarry, then pounced in to kill. Henry
was delighted. He laughed and joked. They had laid
wagers. Then, in turn, the others, Tom included, released their hawks. Henry called the hawk boy to him.
The boy knelt on the grass, and Henry roared, "Don't
kneel, damn you. We are all men out here." He chose
a small merlin and gave her to me, showing me how
to carry her on my wrist. He asked after Latimer's
health. Very assiduously, I told him that he seemed
better, though very tired, and that he was at home
translating a Greek work. Then His Grace asked me
to ride beside him, and he chatted and thanked me
for riding out to Hatfield House to see the children,

Prince Edward and young Bess. He was in high good spirits. He waved his cap, plumes waving, and called out, "We shall meet again, my lady, at Greenwich." He led his party off at a mad gallop, leaving Tom to ride with me and Lucy and a page.

I felt very free from care. Tom took the small hawk from my wrist and gave it to the page, and he, Lucy, and I raced one another up the slope. I felt aware in the dream of a breeze, and joked with Lucy at not having to wear the awful boned corset the women wore then. Tom said that a horse felt good after days at sea, and he was going to Syon house. I felt guilty for being so happy when my husband was at home, ill.

DREAM #2

I was back in the past, at Hampton Court, in what had been Jane's apartments. Katharine Howard had been beheaded months before. In fact, I knew that the King had been alone since her death. I was aware of the year in my dream—1543—and I was a widow; Latimer had died. I felt alone. Tom was in France about the King's affairs, and I wished that he were here. The King had sent for me, and I was afraid that I knew why he had sent for me. There was a noise outside, and the doors were flung open. The King and two gentlemen in waiting came in. I curtsied to him, and His Grace took my arm and raised me, saying to his men, "Leave me, gentlemen, I pray you. I would speak privily with Lady Latimer."

They left, and Henry led me to a window seat. He kissed my hand and held me by the arm, then kissed my cheek and said, "How fair thou art, sweet lady, and kind as thou art comely. Today I was at Hatfield, and my motherless boy told me of your visits." He was in excellent spirits. His rages after Katharine Howard's death were all gone. I felt almost choking with fear, as I knew what was to come, and yet I pitied him. He was a crumbling lion and ruled a turbulent country as only a strong man could. He said, "You could give me much comfort and peace, Madam Kate, and, who knows, perhaps more heirs for England." In the dream I felt at a loss for words. He went on, saying, "My offer does not please you? I thought to do you honor and ask you to wed with me, for truly I have grown to love you very dearly." I told him bluntly, being a North Country woman, that I had not expected this, and, while honored, also felt a little afraid to accept, seeing the fate of two of his queens.

He was not angry, but told me to "have no fear." I had "twice been wed and widowed" and was "known to be virtuous," and that "no scandal could ever attach" to me; that I had "both intellect and gaiety." He asked me to let him know very quickly as time passed and he was aging, but felt for me as any stripling. "Be kind to me. Be kind to England." Now, what woman could resist a proposal like that? Even in a dream of centuries ago? Incidentally, he removed my widow's veil and tossed it on the floor. That was Henry. We walked down the long gallery, and in my dream I knew it was where Katharine Howard had run screaming to try and reach the King. Henry seemed to sense this and told me, "Forget what has gone before." We went into another room he called his closet, and he seemed very gay, almost boyish, and told me that I could refurnish the queen's apartments as I wished; the Exchequer was low, but so be it. I told him (North Country thrift) that I had loved Jane's apartments and hangings, and that I had brocades and hangings in storerooms at Snape if he would like me to use them. He told me I was the first woman who had not sought to ruin him. And that was the end of the dream, all very domestic and practical. I remember, his eyes were small and sunk in heavy jowls, but he still had remnants of his former handsomeness, though he limped. I was aware in the dream of being sad that Tom had not returned in time and that the only way I could refuse the royal offer without offense was to enter a convent, and that did not appeal to me. I also knew it would endanger Tom to refuse Henry and hope to marry Tom later; heads fell for far less.

Mrs. Warren-Browne has, of course, read a few books on the period by now, especially Agnes Strickland's *The Queens of England,* and *Hackett's History of Henry VIII,* but she has not become a scholar on the subject. Perhaps she needn't, having primary access to information scholars have to dig for year after year.

Is Mrs. Catharine Warren-Browne the reincarnated queen of England Katharine Parr, last and happiest of the wives of Henry VIII? She does not claim to be, but I think that the evidence points in that direction. The manner in which the first bits of personal data were received indicates that they came from a source that knew well what the lives of Tom Seymour and Katharine Parr were like. I am satisfied that coincidence, unconscious knowledge, and other ordinary factors do not play a dominant role in this case.

VII

SALLY
AND THE
HIGHWAYMAN

nfinished romantic business or sudden separation of lovers can sometimes lie dormant a long time, until conditions of a psychic kind are right for communication to occur. A person can have all sorts of other psychic experiences, then suddenly the long-ago lover turns up.

During the summer of 1973, I received a strangely elaborate and pleading letter from a young woman by the name of Cynthia von Rupprath-Snitily. The name itself was fascinating enough to warrant my further interest, but what the lady had to say concerning her strange experiences with the unknown would have attracted me even if her name had been Smith or Jones.

Cynthia had been born December 31, 1948, in Chicago, and lived in the same house until twenty-one years of age, leaving the area only to attend college at Northern Illinois University in De Kalb. I immediately recalled my own visit to Northern Illinois University, a huge college set in a very small town in the middle of the Illinois plains, a school that seemed forever to battle the narrow-mindedness of the surrounding town while catering to a very large student body bent on exploring the further reaches of the human mind. Cynthia holds a Bachelor's degree in both history and art, and is an art historian by profession. "I have dealt with both fictitious legend and concrete fact," she stated, "and therefore I have knowledge of the fine lines that sometimes separate these two entities. I have thus carried over the cognizance to my everyday life and have incorporated it into my style of thinking. In truth, I am my own worst critic."

In 1970 she married a man she had met at the University of Notre Dame and moved to his home town of Seattle, Washington, where he was employed at Boeing Aircraft. With the termination of the SST project, her husband enlisted in the Air Force and at the time of contacting me they were stationed at the Edwards Air Force Base in California, about an hour's drive from Los Angeles.

Cynthia had always been a serious and sensitive person, perhaps because she was an only child of parents forty years older than herself. As a result she felt more at ease with older people, preferring their company to that of people her own age. Due to her sensitivity, she was in the habit of becoming rather emotional in matters of impact to her. In order to offset this strong character trait and in view of her profession, she tried very hard to develop a logical and orderly approach to things, and to think matters over several times before taking any specific course of action. Thus, when she realized that she had had psychic experiences from childhood onward and saw them continue in her life, she decided to analyze and investigate the phenomena in which she was a central element. She soon realized that her psychic ability had been inherited from her mother's side of the family; her maternal grandparents had come to the United States from Croatia. Deeply embedded in the culture of many Croatian people is the belief in witchcraft and the ability of some countryfolk to do unusual things or experience the uncanny. But Cynthia's attitude toward these phenomena remained critical. "I am not overwilling to accept such phenomena without further investigation," she explained. One case in particular impressed her, since it involved her personally.

"This case is unusual because it has occurred to three successive generations through the years. In the 1910s my grandmother was living in Chicago performing household tasks, when a neighbor dressed entirely in black came to the door. The latter woman was commonly known as a 'strega' and my grandmother naturally was not too happy to see her. The woman wanted to know what my grandmother was cooking in the pot on the stove. My grandmother refused and told the woman to leave, whereupon the latter reported that she would return that night, 'to find that which she was seeking.' That night while my grandparents, my mother, and my Uncle Bill were all sleeping in the same bed, the door suddenly blew open and my mother recalls seeing my grandmother literally struggling with some unseen force on the bed. Mother remembers quite vividly the movement of the mattress, as if something were jumping up and down on it. Certainly the sensation was stronger than a reclining figure could have inflicted. An aura of evil seemed to have invaded the room and left as quickly as did the 'force.' Years later, at the beginning of 1949, a similar event took place. My aunt was sitting in our Chicago home, feeding me a bottle, when this force again entered the scene, causing the two of us to be considerably uplifted from the couch. Again the jumping persisted and the evil presence was felt. The next performance by this 'thing' occurred in the early months of 1971 in Seattle. It was around midnight and I was reading a novel while my husband, Gary, slept. I suddenly sensed something wicked within the confines of our room. I tossed it off, but then there began that jumping motion. I became quite alarmed as I realized neither my sleeping husband nor my own reclined body could attest to such motion. I woke my husband, who is not psychic, and he, too, became aware of the jumping movement. It was now growing in intensity, but when I called out the Lord's name, the bed suddenly ceased pitching. It wasn't until April 1971, after moving from Seattle, that I learned of the two previous experiences."

On her father's side, Cynthia is descended from a noble German family, originally from Hanover. Her father had no interest in or use for anything psychic. When Cynthia was only a few months old, her Aunt Doris came to live with the family as a temporary replacement for her mother, who was then quite ill and in the hospital. The aunt was sleeping on the living room couch, Cynthia's father in the front bedroom, and Cynthia herself in a crib placed in the back bedroom. Everyone was very much concerned with her mother's health, and her aunt, being Roman Catholic, had been praying almost around the clock. She had only been asleep for a short time when a cold breeze awakened her, and to her amazement she saw a woman, fairly young and dressed in a nun's habit, walk slightly *above* the floor through the living room and turn down the hall toward Cynthia's room. Concerned for the little girl's safety, the aunt quickly followed the woman into the room. There she saw the nun place her hands on Cynthia's crib, look down at her and smile. She seemed quite unaware of the aunt and, her mission apparently accomplished, turned and walked down the hall. The aunt immediately checked the baby, and seeing that the child was all right, went after the apparition. When she arrived at the living room, the figure had vanished, yet there remained a strong scent of roses in the air that even Cynthia's father noticed the following morning. The scent remained in the house, even though it was winter, until Cynthia's mother came home from the hospital. There were no perfume sachets, fresh flowers, or air fresheners that could have accounted for the strange odor. The unusual scent has returned to the house from time to time and can never be satisfactorily explained; it usually coincides with an illness in the family, and has often served as a kind of telepathic warning to Cynthia's mother, when Cynthia was ill while at college. This particular event, of course, was told to Cynthia many years later at a family gathering, but it served to underline Cynthia's own awareness of her unusual faculty.

"Perhaps the most vivid and memorable personal experience occurred to me when I was in grade school," Cynthia explained. "During the 1950s and '60s, I had always heard footsteps starting in the aforementioned living room, coming into the front bedroom and stopping at my bed, both during the day and at night. My parents always attributed the noises to the creaking of old floors, but the house was only built in 1947. At times, the footfalls backed away from the bed, thus disputing the "last footsteps before going to bed" theory. I occupied a twin bed which faced the hallway when the bedroom door was open. On the left side of the bed, my side, was the wall shared by both the living room and front bedroom; Mother slept in the other twin bed adjacent to the driveway wall.

"During one particular night, I had gotten up to go to the bathroom, and upon returning to my bed, snuggled under the covers and shot a quick glance at my sleeping mother. Suddenly, the room became exceptionally cold and on looking toward the door, which I had forgotten to close, I saw four figures coming from the living room *through* the hallway wall and turn into our bedroom. In order to assert that I hadn't unconsciously fallen asleep since returning to bed, I began pinching myself and looking from time to time to the familiar surrounding room and my mother. Thus I know I was fully awake and not dreaming. The first figure entering the room was dressed, as were all the others, in nineteenth-century Western American clothing. She was a woman in her forties of average height, very thin and dressed in a brown-and-white calico dress with high-button collar and long sleeves; her dark brown hair was parted in the middle and tied tightly on top of her head in a bun. There was a prim, austere air about her. She moved to the foot of the bed on my far left. Next came a very tall and lanky man, brown hair parted in the middle, wearing a brown three-piece suit, rather shabby. He took his place in the middle, at the foot of my bed. Following him was a woman whom I felt was out of place, even at the time of the vision. She was dressed in the most outlandish purple satin outfit, tucked up on one side as a barroom girl might have worn in the Old West. Her blonde hair was curled in ringlets, which were drawn up on one side of her head and cascaded down on the other. I sensed loneliness and a very gentle nature surrounding her as she took her place next to the tall gentleman to my right. Lastly came a very dapper if somewhat plump gray-haired gentleman. He carried a small three-legged stool and a black bag, telling me he was probably a medical man. Hatted and wearing a gray three-piece suit complete with gold watch chain, he seated himself on his stool on my right-hand side of the bed. They all seemed terribly concerned over my health, although I was not ill at the time. When the 'doctor' leaned over the bed and tried to take my hand into his, I decided I had experienced just about all I wanted to with these strangers. My voice quivered as I called out to my mother, who was a very light sleeper, and whose back was facing me, informing her of the unknowns who had invaded our bedroom. 'Mother, there are people in the room!' I called again and again. She reassured me sleepily and without turning over that I was only dreaming, and to go back to sleep. During these implorings on my part, the four strangers began backing away from the bed as if they were alarmed by my speaking. Whether they actually spoke or I heard them telepathically, I cannot be certain, but I did 'hear' them repeatedly say, 'No, please, we only want to help you. No, no, don't call out.' My cries increased and with that they turned and exited the same way they had entered, through the wall into the living room."

The house in which this vision took place had only been built in comparatively recent times. The land had formed part of a farm in the early nineteenth century, but the costumes of the figures, Cynthia felt sure, belonged to an earlier period. She wondered whether perhaps the land had been part of a western wagon trail, and she was reliving a child's death. On the other hand, she began to wonder whether it referred to a previous existence of her own, since she has very strong feelings about the nineteenth-century West.

Cynthia has had a number of precognitive dreams concerning events that later took place. But the dream that impressed itself more than any other upon her consciousness had to do with the past. Actually, it was preceded by what she described as "an insatiable interest in England" she developed in early high school. This was not a single dream, easily forgotten, but a series of recurrent dreams, all related to one another, mounting in intensity as if something within her was trying to come to the surface, informing her of a long-forgotten memory.

"At times I noticed myself speaking in a North Country British accent and I caught myself using English spellings, drinking tea with cream, and the first time I heard the song 'Greensleeves' I felt very moved and certainly melancholy. There is another song, called 'North Country Maid,' which has remained my great favorite. I even went so far as to compose a 200-page term paper on England for my sociology class. But long before this project took place, I began dreaming of a cloaked man mounting a horse in the moonlight and riding out of sight into the English countryside. I was in the dream also, dressed in a blue-and-tan peasant frock, laced up the front. I knew it was me because I remember looking down at the dress I was wearing. In other

words, I was actually a participant, not a sleeping specta-
tor of myself, nor recognizing myself as another person.
At any rate, I seemed to be coming out of a stable or
barn, in which I had been lying on a large pile of hay. I
begin running toward the mounting horseman, as if to
beg him not to leave. Then I would awaken, only to
dream the same dream several nights later.

"One night when I was particularly tired, I managed to continue my dream state after the wench's running, but not for long. In the dream, I uttered between
sobs the name of Dick, and then awoke. The dream continued in this pattern until I, now exasperatedly curious, forced myself to remain sleeping. Finally, one
night, I was able to hear the whole phrase—'Dick Turpin, my love, wait! Don't go!' Its mission now seemingly
fulfilled by giving me a name I had never heard before,
the dream never returned again."

At that time, Cynthia had never heard of Dick Turpin. But the dreams had roused her curiosity and she
started to research it. Her Encyclopedia Britannica was
of very little help, nor did any of the high school ency-
clopedias contain the name. But in her parents' library
she located a 1940 edition of Nelson's Encyclopedia. In
it, she found a brief listing of one Richard Turpin, an
English highwayman and associate of Tom King, who
lived from 1706 to 1739, when he was hanged.

About a year after the dreams had subsided, she
was riding with a girlfriend when she suddenly felt a
strong urge to return home immediately. Still under a
kind of compulsion, she immediately turned on the television set and picked a Walt Disney show, very much to
her parents' surprise, since they knew her to dislike the
program. At that moment, flashed on the screen were

the words "The Legend of Dick Turpin." Cynthia then proceeded to watch the program, her eyes glued to the set, interrupting the proceedings on screen with comments of her own. "No, that wasn't what happened," she would say and proceed to correct it. What was remarkable was her ability to relate what was about to happen onscreen and to mention characters' names before this information became available to the viewers. Afterward she felt dazed and remembered little of what she had said during the program.

I suggested that Cynthia meet me in Los Angeles so that I could attempt to regress her hypnotically and determine whether her reincarnation memory was factual or merely a romantic fantasy. We met just before Christmas 1973 at my Hollywood hotel, the Continental Hyatt House. We discussed Cynthia's psychic experiences and I discovered that she had had an accident in 1969 resulting in a brain concussion. Did the accident influence her psychic perceptions in any way? No, she replied, she had had them for years prior to the accident, and they continued after the accident. Had she ever been to England or was she of English background? Both questions she answered in the negative. Her interest in English history and literature at college came *after* the recurrent dream had occurred to her. Having established that neither Cynthia nor her family had any English background nor leanings, I proceeded to regress her hypnotically in the usual manner. It took only a short time before she was under, ready to answer my questions while hypnotized.

After describing life as a Victorian gentleman in New York and giving the name of John Wainscott and the year 1872 or 1892, she proceeded back into the eighteenth century and the year 1703, to a man who had something to do with a Delaware Street. The man's name was Dick, and evidently we had gotten to the subject of her recurrent dreams.

"He is mounting a horse, and he's throwing his cape back so he can take hold of the reins. He's got a hat on with a plume on it, I am standing by the barn."

"What is your relationship with this man? What is your name?" I asked.

"A wench . . . my name is Sally."

"What year is this?"

"1732."

"What happens then?"

"He rides away like he always does."

"What happens to you?"

"I cry."

And that was all I could get out of her through hypnotic regression. But somehow it must have settled this recurrent dream and the urgency connected with it within Cynthia, for I heard nothing further from her after that.

VIII

THE NAKED LADY
OF WOODHOUSE LEA

ust because two lovers are both "dead" does not mean they are together Over There. Especially if one of the two has met a very violent or otherwise traumatic death, and when there is anger and great emotional turmoil involved, getting together again in the next state of existence may prove something of a hassle. What separates the lovers, of course, is the anger of the one who has been hurt. But to forgive in order to get free of it and move on is a very difficult matter indeed.

The case I am about to report concerns a long-ago noblewoman who loved her husband very much indeed. But this happened in Scotland centuries ago, when men were forever fighting and often absent from home. In this case home was a fortified manor house in the hills beyond Edinburgh, and Scotland was rent by many internal disputes and sometimes savage encounters between enemies. The facts behind the story concern one Lady Anne Bothwell, whose husband was absent from the house when one of his mortal enemies, who had waited for just such an opportunity, invaded the house, ransacked it, and forced the lady of the house out into the bitter cold and snow, stark naked. That was his way of getting at her husband, his enemy—a very cowardly way it was indeed. Lady Anne died out there, but her spirit is apparently forever searching for her beloved husband still.

When I was in Edinburgh some years ago researching a book about England and Scotland, I met a group of people who had been to the place and had experienced certain phenomena. After talking with them for a while at a local pub, we decided to see it firsthand.

The discussion of various ghostly events had made the time fly, and suddenly we halted at our destination, Woodhouse Lea. Ian Groat, a gunsmith by profession, had had an uncanny experience here and wanted me to see the place where it all happened. We were on a hill overlooking Edinburgh, and there were a stable and a modern house to our left. Farther up the hill, following the narrow road, one could make out the main house itself. According to my information, Woodhouse Lea had originally stood on another site, farther east, but had been transferred to the present spot. There was a local tradition of a "White Lady of Woodhouse Lea," and it was her appearance that I was after. It was a bitingly cold day for April, so we decided to stay in the car at first while we sorted out Mr. Groat's experiences.

"In January of 1964 I went to Woodhouse Lea in the company of Mr. and Mrs. Peter London," Ian told us. "We waited for several hours in the basement of the house, which had been used to store fodder for horses."

"I gather you went there because of the tradition that a 'White Lady' appeared there?" I asked.

Ian nodded. "After about two hours, a fluorescent light appeared behind one of the doors, which was slightly ajar. It seemed to move backwards and forwards for about five minutes and then disappeared. All three of us saw it. The light was coming from behind that door. We were waiting to see whether anything would actually enter the room, but nothing did, and so we left."

"What was the house like at that point?"

"It was still standing, though several large pieces of masonry had fallen and were lying in front of it. The woodwork was in very poor condition and floorboards were missing, but part of the original grand staircase was still there. It was dangerous to walk in it at night, and even in daylight one had to walk very carefully."

The house could have been restored, if someone had wanted to foot the expense. For a while the monument commission thought of doing it, but nothing came of it, and eventually the owners pulled it down. The decision was made in a hurry, almost as if to avoid publicity about the destruction of this historical landmark. It was all done in one weekend. The masonry and what was still standing was pulled down by heavy machinery, then stamped into the ground to serve as a kind of base for the modern chalet the owners of the land built on top of it. It reminded me of some of the barbarous practices going on in the United States of pulling down old landmarks in order to build something new and, preferably, profitable.

Peter London was shocked at the sudden disappearance of the old mansion house, and he got to talking to some of the girls working in the stables at the bottom of the hill, also part of the estate. Several of them had seen the apparition of a woman in white.

The strange thing is that the British army had invested seven thousand pounds in central heating equipment when they occupied the building during World War II, when the building was still in pretty good shape.

"During the war there was a prisoner-of-war camp that bordered on the actual Woodhouse Lea Estate," Ian continued. "The sentries kept a log of events, and there are fourteen entries of interest, stretching over a three-year period. These concerned sightings of a 'woman in white' who was challenged by the sentries. Incidentally, the stable girls saw her walking about the grounds, *outside* the house, not in the house itself or in the stables."

I decided it was time to pay a visit to the area where the mansion last stood. Since there had been no time to make arrangements for my investigation, Mr. Groat went ahead, and to our pleasant surprise he returned quickly, asking us to come inside the stable office, at the bottom of the hill. There we were received by a jolly gentleman who introduced himself as Cedric Burton, manager of the estate. I explained the purpose of my visit. In Scotland, mentioning ghosts does not create any great stir: they consider it part of the natural phenomena of the area.

"As I know the story," Mr. Burton said, "her name was Lady Anne Bothwell, and originally she lived at the *old* Woodhouse Lea Castle, which is about four miles from here. Once when her husband was away, one of his enemies took over the castle and pushed her out, and she died in the snow. I gather she appears with nothing on at all when she does appear. That's the way she was pushed out—naked. Apparently her ghost made such a nuisance of itself that the owners decided to move the castle and brought most of the stones over here and built the mansion house called Woodhouse Lea up on the hill. The last person I know of who heard a manifestation was a coachman named Sutherland, and that was just before electric light was installed. There has been no sign of her since."

"I gather there were a number of reports. What exactly did these people see?"

"Well, it was always the same door on the north side of the building, and on snowy nights there was a fairly vigorous knock on the door; and when someone would go outside to investigate, there was never anyone there —nor were there any footprints in the deep snow. That, I think, was the extent of the manifestations, which are of course tremendously exaggerated by the local people. Some say it is a White Lady, and one has even heard people coming up the drive. I've heard it said, when the old house was standing there empty, lights were seen in the rooms."

"Has the house ever been seriously investigated?"

"Some Edinburgh people asked permission and sat in the old house at midnight on midsummer's eve. However, I pointed out to them that she was only known to appear around seven in the evening and in deep snow. Midnight on midsummer's eve wasn't the most auspicious occasion to expect a manifestation. There was another chap who used to bring his dog up and stand there with his torch from time to time, to see if the dog was bristling."

"When did the actual event occur—the pushing out of the woman?"

"The house was moved to this spot in the early fifteenth century. It was originally built around the old Fulford Tower. It is a bit confusing, because up there also by the house there is an archway built from stones from an entirely different place with the date 1415 on it. This comes from the old Galaspas Hospital in Edinburgh."

"If Woodhouse Lea was moved from the original site to this hill in the early fifteenth century, when was the original house built?"

"Sometime during the Crusades, in the thirteenth century."

While the early history of Woodhouse Lea is shrouded in mystery, there was a Lord Woodhouse Lea in the eighteenth century, a well-known literary figure in Edinburgh. Many other literary figures stayed at the house, including Sir Walter Scott, Alan Ramsey, and James Hogg. Evidently Sir Walter Scott knew that *old* Woodhouse Lea was haunted, because he mentions it in one of his books, and Scottish travel books of the eighteenth century commonly refer to it as 'haunted Woodhouse Lea.' In 1932 control of the house passed into the hands of the army, and much damage was done to the structure. The army held onto it for thirty years.

"Have there been any manifestations reported in recent years?"

"Not really," Mr. Burton replied. "When the bulldozer pulled down the old house, we told people as a joke that the ghost would be trying to burrow her way out of the rubble. Some of the stones from the old house have been incorporated into the new chalet, built on top of the crushed masonry, to give it a sort of continuity."

The chalet is the property of George Buchanan

Smith, whose family uses it as a holiday house. He is the son of Lord Balonough, and his younger brother is the undersecretary of state for foreign affairs in Scotland.

"The house has been talked about tremendously," Mr. Burton said. "It has even been described as the second most haunted house in Scotland. Also, Woseley is not too far from here, and it too has a nude white lady. She has been observed running on the battlements."

"Why did they move the house from the old site to this spot?"

"Because of her. She disturbed them too much."

"And did the manifestations continue on the new site?"

"Yes," Mr. Burton acknowledged. "She came with the stones."

He turned the office over to an assistant and took us up to the chalet. The owner was away, so there was no difficulty in walking about the house. It is a charmingly furnished modern weekend house, with a bit of ancient masonry incorporated into the walls here and there. I gazed at a particularly attractive stone frieze over the fireplace. Inscribed upon it, in Latin, were the words OCCULTUS NON EXTINCTUS: The occult is not dead (just hidden).

IX

SEXUAL POSSESSION FROM THE GREAT BEYOND

When someone—usually, but not always, a woman—is being forced into sexual relations with another person against her will, that is generally considered a case of rape. Even when the other party is someone known to the victim, such as a husband, lover, or would-be lover, the act of coercion still qualifies the attempt as rape.

When it comes to physical contact between a flesh-and-blood person and someone who has died but has nevertheless retained strong feelings and energies, chances are the attentions are unwelcome, though not always.

In this chapter and some of the following ones, I will report true, verified cases of these kinds. Be assured they are not the figments of imagination of frustrated individuals or hallucinations of the psychologically unsound. All of the people to whom these things happened were perfectly sound of body and mind, and they did not "look" for the kind of far-out attention they received, preferring relationships on *this* side of life. This kind of sexual possession by a dead person upon a living one is not very common, but enough cases have been verified to establish its validity.

When someone dies unexpectedly or in the prime of physical life and finds it impossible to express sexual appetite physically in the world into which he or she has been suddenly catapulted, he or she may indeed look around for someone through whom to express this appetite on the earth plane. It is then merely a matter of searching out opportunities, regardless of personalities involved. It is conceivable that a large percentage of the unexplained or inexplicable sexual attacks by otherwise meek, timid, sexually defensive individuals upon members of the opposite sex—or even the same sex—may be due to sudden possession by an entity of this kind. This is even harder to prove objectively than are some of the murder cases involving individuals who do not recall what they have done and are for all practical purposes normal human beings before and after the crime. But I am convinced that the influence of discarnates can indeed be exercised upon proper vehicles—that is to say, appropriately mediumistic individuals. It also appears from my studies that the most likely recipients of this doubtful honor are those who are sexually weak or inactive. Evidentally the unused sexual energies are particularly useful to the discarnate entities for their own gains. There really doesn't seem to be any way in which one can foretell such attacks or prevent them, except, perhaps, by leading a sexually healthy and balanced life. Those who are fulfilled in their natural drives on the earth plane are least likely to suffer from such invasions.

On the other hand, there exist cases of sexual possession involving two partners who knew each other before on the earth plane. One partner was cut short by death, either violently or prematurely, and would now seek to continue a pleasurable relationship of the flesh from the new dimension. Deprived of a physical body to express such desires, however, the deceased partner would then find it rather difficult to express the physical desires to the partner remaining on the earth plane. A sexual relationship takes two, and if the remaining partner is not willing then difficulties will have to be reckoned with.

An interesting case came to my attention a few months ago. Mrs. Anna C. lives with her several children in a comparatively new house in the northeastern United States. She bought the house eighteen months after her husband passed away. Thus there was no connection between the late husband and the new house. Nevertheless, her husband's passing was by no means the end of their relationship. "My husband died five years ago this past September. Ever since then he has not let me have a peaceful day," she explained in desperation, seeking my help. Two months after her husband had died she saw him coming to her in a dream complaining that she had buried him alive. He explained that he wasn't really dead, and that it was all her fault and her family's fault that he died in the first place. Mr. C. had lived a rather controversial life, drinking regularly and frequently staying away from home. Thus the relationship between himself and his wife was far from ideal. Nevertheless, there was a strong bond between them. "In other dreams he would tell me that *he was going to have sex relations with me, whether I wanted him to or not.* He would try to grab me and I would run all through the house with him chasing after me. I never let him get hold of me. He was like that when he was alive, too. The most important thing in life to him was sex and he didn't care how or where he got it. Nothing else mattered to him," she complained, describing vividly how the supposedly dead husband apparently still had a great deal of life in him. "He then started climbing on the bed and walking up and down on it and scaring me half to death. I didn't know what it was or what to do about it," she said, trembling.

When Mr. C. could not get his wife to cooperate willingly, he apparently got mad. To express his displeasure, he caused all sorts of havoc around the household. He would tear a pair of stockings every day for a week, knock things over, and even go to the place where his mother-in-law worked as a cook, causing seemingly inexplicable phenomena to occur there as well. When an aunt in Indiana tried to get rid of him and his influences by performing a spiritualist ritual at the house, he appeared to her to tell her to mind her own business and stay out of his personal relationship with Mrs. C. Meanwhile Mr. C. amused himself by setting alarm clocks to go off at the wrong times or stopping them altogether, moving objects from their accustomed places or making them disappear altogether, only to return them several days later to everyone's surprise. In general, he behaved like a good poltergeist should. But it didn't endear him any more to his erstwhile wife.

When Mrs. C. rejected his attentions, he started to try to possess his ten-year-old daughter. He came to her in dreams and told her that her mother wasn't really knowledgeable about anything. He tried everything in his power to drive a wedge between the little girl and her mother. As a result of this, the little girl turned more and more away from her mother, and no matter how Mrs. C. tried to explain things to her, she found the little girl's mind made up under the influence of her late father.

In a fit of destructiveness, the late Mr. C. then started to work on the other children, creating such a state of havoc in the household that Mrs. C. did not know where to turn any longer. Then the psychic aunt from Indiana came to New England to try and help matters. Sure enough, Mr. C. appeared to her and the two had a cozy talk. He explained that he was very unhappy where he was and was having trouble getting along with the people over there. To this the aunt replied she would be very happy to help him get to a higher plane if that was what he wanted. But that wasn't it, he replied. He just wanted to stay where he was. The aunt left for home. Now the children, one by one, would become unmanageable, and Mrs. C. assumed that her late husband was interfering with their proper education and discipline. "I am fighting an unseen force and cannot get through to the children," she explained.

Her late husband did everything to embarrass her. She was working as a clerk at St. Francis's rectory in her town, and doing some typing. It happened to be December 24, 1971, Christmas Eve. All of a sudden she heard a thud in her immediate vicinity and looked down to the floor. A heavy dictionary that had been on the shelf only a fraction of a second before was lying at her feet. A co-worker wondered what was up. She was hard pressed to explain the presence of the dictionary on the floor, since it had been on the shelf in back of them only a moment before. But she knew very well how the dictionary came to land there.

Evidently Mr. C. had prepared special Christmas surprises for his wife. She went to her parents' house to spend the holiday. During that time her nephew George was late for work since his alarm had not worked properly. It turned out that someone had stuck a pencil right through the clock. As soon as the pencil was removed, the clock started to work again. On investigation it turned out that no one had been near the clock, and when the family tried to place the pencil into the clock, as they had found it, no one could do it. The excitement made Mrs. C. so ill she went to bed. That was no way to escape Mr. C.'s attentions, however. The day before New Year's Eve, her late husband got to her, walking up and down on the bed itself. Finally she told him to leave her and the children alone, to go where he belonged. She didn't get an answer.

Phenomena continued in the house, so she asked her aunt to come back once again. This time the aunt from Indiana brought oil with her and put it on each of the children and Mrs. C. herself. Apparently it worked, or so it seemed to Mrs. C. But her late husband was merely changing his tactics. A few days later she was sure that he was trying to get into one of the children to express himself further since he could no longer get at her. She felt she would be close to a nervous breakdown if someone could not help her get rid of the phenomena and—above all—break her husband's hold on her. "I am anxious to have him sent on up where he can't bother anyone any more," she explained.

Since I could not go immediately, and the voice on the telephone sounded as if its owner could not hold out a single day more, I asked Ethel Johnson Meyers, my mediumistic friend, to go out and see what she could do.

Mrs. C. had to go to Mrs. Meyers' house for a personal sitting first. A week later Ethel came down to Mrs. C.'s house to continue her work. What Mrs. Meyers discovered was somewhat of a surprise to Mrs. C. and to myself. It was her contention that the late husband, while still in the flesh, had himself been the victim of possession and had done the many unpleasant things (of which he was justly accused) during his lifetime, not of his own volition but under the direction of another entity. That the possessor was himself possessed seemed like a novel idea to me, one neither Mrs. Meyers nor I could prove. Far more important was the fact that Mrs. Meyers' prayers and commands to the unseen entity seemed to have worked, for he walks up and down Mrs. C.'s bed no more, and all is quiet.

X

THE CASE
OF THE SPURNED
LOVER

In olden days, cases like this one would immediately be blamed on the devil himself because science had not yet come to grips with the paranormal. Even in this so-called enlightened age, there are fanatics who prefer belief in the devil to the acceptance of unusual but nevertheless real situations that run counter to what they have grown up with.

If you live in Kansas City you're bound to hear about the devil now and again if you are a Bible student or a member of a church that goes in for the hell-and-brimstone variety of preaching. To some people the devil is real and they will give you an argument filled with fervor and Bible quotations to prove that he exists.

Mrs. G. wasn't one of those who were impressed by demonic outbursts, however, and could not care less whether there was a devil or not. She had grown up in a well-to-do middle-class family and spent her adult years in the world of business. At age nineteen, she met and married Mr. G. and they have had a happy life together ever since. There are no children, no problems, no difficulties whatever. She was always active in her husband's gasoline business, and only lately had she decided to slow down a little, and perhaps do other things, leisure-time things, or just plain nothing when the mood would strike her.

At age forty-nine that was a pretty good way to do things, she figured, and since she really did not have to work, it was just as well that she started to enjoy life a little more fully. Not that she was unhappy or frustrated in any way, but after thirty years of living with the gasoline business longed for some fresh air.

One day in the spring of 1964, a friend suggested something new and different for them to do. She had read an advertisement in the local paper that had intrigued her. A Spiritualist church was inviting the general public to its message service. Why didn't they have a look?

"Spiritualist church?" Mrs. G. asked with some doubt. She really did not go for that sort of thing. And yet, way back in her early years, she had had what are now called ESP experiences. When she talked to a person, she would frequently know what that person would answer before the words were actually spoken. It scared the young girl, but she refused to think about it. Her parents' home was a twelve-year-old house in a good section of Kansas City. It was just a pleasant house without any history of either violence or unhappiness. And yet she would frequently hear strange raps at night, raps that did not come from the pipes or other natural sources. Whenever she heard those noises she would simply turn to the wall and pretend she did not hear them, but in her heart she knew they were there.

Then one night she was awakened from deep sleep

by the feeling of a presence in her room. She sat up in bed and looked out. There, right in front of her bed, was the kneeling figure of a man with extremely dark eyes in a pale face. Around his head he wore a black and white band, and he was dressed in a togalike garment with a sash, something from another time and place, she thought. She rubbed her eyes and looked again, but the apparition was gone.

Before long, she had accepted the phenomenon as simply a dream, but again she knew this was not so and she was merely accommodating her sense of logic. But who had the stranger been? Surely the house was not haunted. Besides, she did not believe in ghosts.

As a young woman, she once heard a friend in real estate talk about selling a haunted house not far from them. She thought this extremely funny and kidded her friend about it often. Little did she know at the time how real this subject was yet to become in her later years!

The haunted house across the street was sold, incidentally, but nothing further was heard about it, so Mrs. G. assumed the new owners did not care or perhaps weren't aware of whatever it was that was haunting the premises. Her own life had no room for such matters, and when her friend suggested they attend the Spiritualist church meeting, she took it more as a lark than a serious attempt to find out anything about the hereafter.

They went that next night, and found the meeting absorbing, if not exactly startling. Perhaps they had envisioned a Spiritualist meeting more like a séance with dark windows and dim lights and a circle of hand-holding believers, but they were not disappointed in the quality of the messages. Evidently some of those present did receive proof of survival from dear departed ones, even though the two women did not. At least not to their satisfaction. But the sincere atmosphere pleased them and they decided to come back again on another occasion.

At the meeting they overheard a conversation between two members. "He came through to me on the ouija board," one lady said, and the other nodded in understanding.

A ouija board? That was a toy, of course. No serious-minded individual would take such a tool at face value. Mrs. G. had more time than ever on her hands and the idea of "playing around" with the ouija board tickled her fancy. Consequently she bought a board the following week and decided she would try it whenever she had a moment all to herself.

That moment came a few days later, when she was all by herself in the house. She placed her fingers lightly on the indicator, the plastic arrow designed to point at individual letters to spell out words. Mrs. G. was positive that only her own muscle power could move the indicator but she was willing to be amused that afternoon and was, so to speak, game for whatever might come through the board.

Imagine her surprise when the board began to throb the moment she placed her hands upon it. It was a distinct, intense vibration, similar to the throbbing of an idling motor. As soon as she lifted her hands off the board, it stopped. When she replaced them, it began again after about a minute or two, as if it were building up energy again. She decided there was nothing very alarming in all this and that it was probably due to some natural cause, very likely energy drawn from her body.

After a moment, her hands began to move across

the board. She assured herself that she was not pushing the indicator knowingly but there was no doubt she was being compelled to operate the indicator by some force outside herself!

Now her curiosity got the upper hand over whatever doubts she might have had at the beginning of the "experiment," and she allowed the indicator to rush across the board at ever-increasing speed. As the letters spelled out words she tried to remember them, and stopped from time to time to write down what had been spelled out on the board.

"Hello," it said, "this is John W."

She gasped and let the pencil drop. John W. was someone she knew well. She had not thought of him for many years and if his name was still imbedded in her unconscious mind, it had been dormant for so long and so deeply, she could scarcely accuse her own unconscious of conjuring him up now.

John W. had worshiped her before she was married. Unfortunately, she had not been able to return the feeling with the same intensity. Ultimately they lost track of each other and in thirty years never saw each other again. She learned from mutual acquaintances, however, that he had also got married and settled down in a nice house not far from where she and Mr. G. lived. But despite this proximity, she never met him nor did she feel any reason to.

John W. was also in the gasoline business, so they did have that in common, but there had been difficulties between them that had made a marriage undesirable from her point of view. He was a good man but somehow not her "type," and she never regretted having turned him down, although she supposed he did not take it lightly at the time. But so many years had passed that time would have healed whatever wounds there might have been then.

When John W. died of heart failure in 1964 he was in his late fifties. Over the years he had developed a morbid personality and it had overshadowed his former carefree self.

"Hello," the ouija board communicator had said, "this is John W."

Could it be? she wondered. She put the board away in haste. Enough for now, she thought.

But then her curiosity made her try it again. As if by magic, the indicator flew over the board.

"I want to be with you, always," the board spelled out now. And then a very avalanche of words followed, all of them directed toward her, telling her how much he had always loved and wanted her.

Could this be something made up in her own unconscious mind? Why would she subject herself to this incursion? For an incursion it soon turned out to be. Practically every day she found herself drawn to the ouija board. For hours she would listen to the alleged John W. tell her how much he wanted to stay with her now that he had found her again. This was punctuated with bitter complaints that she had hurt him, that she had not understood his great devotion for her.

As the weeks went by, her own personality changed and she began to take on more and more of his characteristic moods. She turned moody and morbid and her husband could not fail to notice the change that had come over his wife. But she did not feel she could tell him what had happened, partly because she did not really believe it herself yet, and partly because she felt it might harm their marriage. So she pretended to be depressed and her husband understood, blaming her middle years for it.

By the winter of 1964, her life was no longer her own. In addition to the frequent ouija board sessions, she now began to hear the man's voice *directly*. "I am with you," he explained fervently, and with her he was. There was never a moment where she could be sure he was not nearby. Her privacy was gone. She kept hearing his voice, sad but nevertheless his voice as it had been in life, talking to her from somewhere outside, and yet seemingly inside her head at the same time. She could not understand any of this and she did not know how to cope with it at first.

She threw away the accursed ouija board that had opened the floodgates to the invasion from the beyond. But it did not help much. He was there, always present, and he could communicate with her through her own psychic sense. She found it difficult to fall asleep. About that time she noticed she was no longer alone in bed. At first she thought it was her imagination, spurred on by fear, that made her *think* the undesired one was with her. But she soon felt his physical presence close to her body.

One night she extended her hand and clearly felt *something* other than air above her own body! She let out a scream and turned on the light. But this merely woke her husband and she had to explain it as a bad dream so that he would not be alarmed.

Night after night, she felt John W.'s ethereal body next to or on top of hers. There was no mistake about it. He was trying to make love to her from the shadowy world he was in, something he had been denied while in the flesh. She fought off his advances as best she could, but it did not deter him in the least.

At the beginning of their communication with the board's help, she had still felt a kind of compassion for the poor devil who had died so sadly and rather early in his life. But whatever positive feelings she still harbored for him soon turned into pure hate. Nothing mattered in her life but to rid herself of this nightmare and return to the placid life she had been leading prior to the incident with the ouija board.

John W. added threats and intimidation to his arsenal of evil now, threats as to what he would do to her and her husband if she did not accept him willingly. Ultimately she could not bear it any longer and decided to inform her husband of what she was going through. At first she was fearful as to what he might say. Perhaps he would have her committed to an institution, or at best subject her to the humiliating treatments of a private psychiatrist.

But her husband listened quietly and with compassion.

"Terrible," he finally commented, "we've got to get you out of this somehow."

She sighed with relief. He evidently believed her. She herself had moments now where she questioned her own sanity. Could such things as the sexual invasion of a woman by a dead man really be? Was she not merely acting out her own suppressed desires due perhaps to middle-age change of life?

She went to seek the advice of a physician. After a careful checkup, he found her physically sound but suggested a psychiatric examination and possibly an EEG—an electroencephalogram to determine brain damage, if any. None of these tests showed anything abnormal. After a while, she concluded that medicine men could not help her even if they should believe her story.

Meanwhile, the attacks became worse. "You will always hear my voice," he promised her night and day, "You won't be able to get rid of me now."

She tried all sorts of things. Grabbing whatever books on the subject of possession she could find, she tried to learn whether others had suffered similar attacks. She tried her skill at automatic writing hoping that it might give the accursed ghost a chance to express himself and perhaps she might reason with him that way. But though she became a proficient automatist, it did not do any good. The handwriting she wrote in was not hers. What she wrote down made no sense to her, but it was he who was using her in still one more way and so she stopped it.

One night she felt him closer than ever. It was as if part of his body were entering hers, and suddenly she felt her heart being squeezed and she gasped for breath. For a few moments of agonizing fear, she felt herself dying of a heart attack. The next day she went to see her doctor again. Her heart was sound as could be. But she knew then that she had just relived the very moment of his death. He had died of just such a heart failure!

Clearly John W. was a disturbed personality in the in-between world in which he now existed after a fashion. He could not distinguish right from wrong, nor indeed recognize his true status. His hatred and love at once kept him glued to her body and her environment, unwilling and unable to break what must have been his strongest desire at the time of death. During their courtship, he had appeared as a good person, unselfish and kind. Now he seemed bitter and full of selfish desire to own her, unwilling to let her go or do anything she asked him to.

She enlisted the help of a local amateur hypnotist, but he failed to put her under hypnosis. Discouraged, she lost all desire to live if it meant living on with this monstrous person inside her.

One day she saw a television program on hypnotic treatment in parapsychological cases. Again encouraged, she asked for help and went to New York for an attempt to dislodge the unwanted entity from her body and soul. This time she did go under, although not very deeply. But it was enough for the personality of John W. to emerge and carry on a conversation of sorts with the hypnotist.

"I want her to go with me, she is all I have now," he said, speaking through Mrs. G.'s mouth in trance.

Later she confirmed that she had been on the brink of suicide recently, and this had not been in a moment of panic but as if someone had actually made her attempt it. Luckily, she had managed to pull out of it just in time.

"Do you believe in a God?" the hypnotist asked.

"No," the entity replied and brushed the question aside. "I told her, she made life hell for me, now I'll make her life hell for her."

"But why do that?"

"No one wants me—I want to cry—you don't know what this is like—over here—nothing but darkness—"

Tears came down Mrs. G.'s cheeks now.

"It's me crying, not *her*," the voice of John W. said, and then, somewhat quieter, "No one wanted me as a child . . . I came from an orphanage . . . my grandparents never wanted me . . . she could have made me happy but she didn't want to. She's the only woman who would have made me happy, only her, but she doesn't want me."

"Then why force yourself on her? What is the point?"

"I force myself on her because I can make her miserable."

"You can't force love."

"I have no pride."

"Renounce her."

"I don't want to listen to you. She hates me now anyway. I'm going to take her with me . . . I'll get her, one way or another, I'll get her all right."

The hypnotist patiently explained about the freedom of the Other Side and how to get there by wishing oneself with one's loved ones who have preceded one.

"This is all new to me," the confused entity replied, but seemed for a moment to be thinking it over.

But it was only a brief squint at the light, then darkness took over once again.

"I've made her cry . . . miserable . . . she made me miserable. I don't like the way she's lived her life. . . ."

Suddenly, the personality seemed to squirm as if from guilt.

Was this his own private hell he was in?

"I'm not really that person . . . I've been lying to her . . . just so I can be around her, I tell her one thing and then another. . . ."

"Then why not leave her and go on to the Other Side?"

"I want to but don't know how—I can't go without *her.*"

The hypnotist tried again, explaining that other souls had been equally confused and been helped "across" the Great Divide.

The voice of the possessing entity hesitated. He was willing to go, but could he see Mrs. G. now and again? Visiting privileges, the hypnotist thought, with a bitter sense of humor.

"Will I be able to come back and see her?" the voice asked again.

But then the demented mind emerged triumphant.

"She hates me for what I've done to her. I'm not going to leave. I can do anything with her. Never could do it when living."

Now the hypnotist dropped the polite approach.

"You are to leave this woman," he intoned, "on pain of eternal damnation."

"I won't go."

"You will be in hell."

"She will be with me then."

"I send you away, the psychic door is closed. You cannot return."

"I will."

A moment later, Mrs. G. awoke, somewhat dumbfounded and tired, but otherwise no worse off than she had been when she had been put under by the hypnotist.

After she returned to Kansas City, she had some hopes that the power of John W. had been broken. But the molesting continued unabated. True, there had been conversation and the entity now knew at least that he was committing a moral offense. But evidently it did not matter to him, for the attacks continued.

After a while, Mrs. G. realized that her anxiety and abject fear were contributing to John W.'s unholy powers. She learned that negative emotions can create energies that can be used by entities such as John W. and when she realized this, her attitude began to change.

Where she had been waiting for his attacks to occur and counting the moments when she was totally free from his possession, she now deliberately disregarded all he did and treated his presence with utter indifference. She could still feel the rage within him when he wanted to possess her, but it was slowly cooling. Gradually her compassion for the bedeviled soul returned and as it did, his hold upon her weakened. He had made his point, after all, and now the point no longer mattered. When last heard from, Mrs. G. was living quietly in Kansas City.

XI

DEAD, BUT NOT GONE

icture this: a healthy young medical doctor goes to Vietnam to serve his country, and experience the terrible nightmare that was the war in Vietnam. But he dies, in the prime of his life. He is not prepared for the sudden change, and his vitality is still intact. He remembers a woman he fancied back home in America and he contacts her. Only he wants more than simple contact.

I was brought into the case of psychic Edith Berger because the people who were handling it were at wit's end. There was the fine medium, the late Betty Ritter, who in turn had been brought into the case by the late psychiatrist Dr. Nandor Fodor, who could no longer deal with it alone. He had been to the house in the company of Betty Ritter, with whom I also worked, and despite their visit and attempted exorcism, the phenomena continued. Betty had suggested that he get in touch with me and that I join the case.

Apparently Edith had known Dr. Bill P. (not his real name), a medical explorer, and had admired his work greatly. The day after his death abroad the young woman discovered that her one-time suitor had attached himself to her and was physically forcing himself on her. The attacks, her mother explained, were so violent that for a while she had to sleep in the same bed with her daughter to protect her. But it did not help. Even the mother felt the physical contact experienced through her daughter. The father of the young woman, a carpenter of Swedish extraction, had been highly skeptical of the entire matter, ascribing it to female hysteria. But even he had to admit that his daughter's behavior changed radically after the phenomena began. Although she had been far from tidy, and had been devoted to a prospective career as a singer, she now became the very model of tidiness and was interested only in being a nurse. It was that profession her late boyfriend had wanted her to pursue. The discarnate doctor was constantly invading Edith's privacy. He expressed himself through her and regulated her life. At times she would even assume the symptoms of the disease from which he had died. She showed evidence of suffering from malaria, yet when examined by a doctor was found to be completely healthy.

One might argue that such exhibitions could be of hysterical origin. Nevertheless they are extraordinary when considered in conjunction with all the other unusual personality changes that happened at the same time. Over and over, the dead doctor asked Edith to tell his mother that he was still alive. But how could she do this and not be labeled insane? In her somewhat simple, devoted way, Edith prayed for his release. It all had begun one day when she was praying for him. She felt a clutching sensation on her arm. Someone was close to

her. A little later she went to bed. It was then that she
heard his voice, speaking to her, "It is I, Bill." The indirect impressions, the personality changes, were followed
by more direct attacks upon her. He wanted to be her
lover as well. On one particular amorous occasion, her
mother reported that she saw a man's outline in the
empty bed. Yet she knew that no man had slept with her
daughter. Quickly the mother grabbed a fly swatter and
hit the outline in the bed. Once when Edith was about to
put on her overcoat she saw it come toward her of its
own volition, as if someone were holding it for her to
slip her arm into. Whenever she was with other men she
felt the dead doctor close to her, kissing her and complaining in a jealous voice that only she could hear.

On her first visit to the house, Betty Ritter immediately contacted the possessing personality and argued
with him. It lessened the late doctor's hold upon Edith,
but he stuck around, now filled with anger as well as
love. The same night Betty Ritter awoke from a restless
sleep to see a man standing next to her bed. He was
stark naked and in a menacing mood. Evidently he had
come to chase *her* away, since the medium had tried to
do the same thing to him earlier that evening. But Betty
Ritter was nonplussed. She prayed and asked her own
"controls" for help. The naked man vanished. Several
days later the medium saw the man again, this time
wearing riding clothes. On inquiry it developed that he
had been a great horseman, and that a riding habit was
one of his favorite costumes. Even while Betty Ritter was
speaking to Edith Berger on the telephone, the impa-
tient possessor started to pull Edith's hair in a most
painful fashion, as if to prove that he was still very much
around.

The possession continued since the doctor, who had died in the prime of life, could not accept the separation from his physical body any more than the separation from his love. It was then that I was called into the case and, together with Dr. Fodor and Betty Ritter, went to the Berger home. This time the entity took over Betty Ritter's unconscious mind almost immediately. Pointing a hand toward Edith, he yelled through the vocal apparatus of Betty Ritter, "I shall not be pulled away from you. I won't go." I began to reason with the entity, both rationally and emotionally, and eventually I must have gotten through to him. He broke down, crying, "I haven't been able to finish what I started," and spoke of his important medical work. After I had explained to him that he could very well continue his research on his side of life without possessing the physical body of his lady friend over here, he understood, and he promised not to trouble her any further. He only asked that he might from time to time be permitted to visit with her, and that I gladly allowed. Nothing further was heard from Edith Berger.

XII

THE HUNGARIAN HUSBAND

ood morning," said the wife of the German magazine editor as she put a pot of boiling coffee before him. "Here's the mail."

Herr Geisler, editor of the German-language magazine *Die Andere Welt* (The Other World), quickly glanced through the stack of letters. Ever since he had announced that I would be coming to Germany to look into some *Spukfaelle* (hauntings), he had been inundated with letters from people who had complaints along those lines. A lot of the letters were the kind you couldn't really sink your teeth into because the experiences were all personal and individual. And there was a small but weird fringe of disturbed people writing in about psychic experiences that were obviously more psychotic than psychic. Nevertheless, Herr Geisler took his mail call seriously, for the reader is the boss with any good magazine editor.

After he had disposed of the more obvious inquiries he finally turned his attention to the mail inquiring about my coming. There was one in particular that stood out from the rest by the firm, determined hand-writing on the envelope.

Without being an expert at graphology, editor Geisler took it for the hand of a young woman or ma-tron. It looked rational and direct and had none of the earmarks of the disturbed individual—people's hand-writing often gives away their mental states.

Imagine Herr Geisler's feelings when he opened the letter and read the message. *Ja,* that was something for Hans Holzer all right.

After he reread the letter to make sure he had not imagined its contents, he sent it off to me with the sug-gestion that I look into the case. The letter, dated May 13, 1966, referred to the announcement of my coming, and then continued:

"For years I have been plagued by a spook. I have recognized the ghost as my husband, wearing a pair of black pants and a white shirt. I should be much obliged to you if you could arrange to have me freed of this spook. I am eighty-four years old and I like to sleep at night."

Anyone who writes that clearly and precisely at age eighty-four deserved my help, I decided. I wrote Mrs. Anna S. a brief note informing her of my coming to Hamburg, at which time I would drive out into the sub-urbs to see and, if possible, to help her.

In July 1966 my wife and I were in Hamburg, where the local television people had requested an in-terview. My book *Ghost Hunter* had recently come out in German, and because of this I had consented. But they wanted more: to cover an actual investigation by me.

I had some misgivings about it as I did not know how seriously they would treat the subject, but finally I

overcame my suspicions and arranged for the Hamburg
TV people to accompany us on the visit to Mrs. S. in a
suburb of Hamburg called Lurup. Naturally I had asked
the lady if it was all right to film my visit and she had not
minded.

We tried very hard to discourage newspapers and
just plain curious people, for I wanted to protect the
privacy of Mrs. S., but when a big, white TV film truck
parks in front of a modern, nondescript apartment
building where there is little that is newsworthy, people
naturally wonder. We unpacked the gear as quickly as
possible—there was a total of five technicians and re-
porters with us—and then walked up to the apartment
occupied by Mrs. S. The old lady meanwhile had
watched the whole procedure calmly from her window.

Rather than upset her by having all seven people
walk in at once, I used an old method previously tried
out with a case in Pittsburgh. First two people come up
and start to chat. Five minutes later, another two ring
the bell and are introduced, and finally you wonder
where are so and so—you need them to be present—
and just about then the door bell rings and there they
are. By that time the subject has gotten used to the idea
of a full house and all proceeds according to plan.

In this case we were met at the door by a smiling,
gray-haired woman who belied her years, rapidly moving about and speaking without the slightest hesitation.
I detected a strange accent in her voice, foreign to the
North German dialect of Hamburg. She later told us she
was Hungarian by birth—no wonder the vivacious tem-
perament was not compatible with the placid North
German character!

"What was the first thing you found unusual?" I

began the interview. We were seated around a nice, middle-class table covered with a nice, middle-class tablecloth.

"The whole thing started in my kitchen," Mrs. S. began, "at all hours, too. Noises, noises—and nobody there. Then one night I was still lying on my bed—I don't sleep an awful lot—waiting for sleep to come. I looked up, and there is my late husband, wearing his black pants and white shirt."

That, of course, was most upsetting to Mrs. S., inasmuch as her husband had been dead and buried for the past twelve years—since 1944 to be exact.

It appeared that Mr. S. had shared her bed and board for only two years of married bliss. Then a local railroad train brought their idyllic existence to a sudden stop—flagged down, you might say. Mr. S. worked on the railroad, and he had come to the end of his line. Or so Mrs. S. had thought until the racket started up in her kitchen. "Especially my closet," she emphasized. "That's where he stays."

It didn't seem right for a man of the road like Mr. S. to be cooped up in a kitchen closet, but Mrs. S. assured me there was little doubt about it. Regular knocks would announce his presence, and others had heard them too.

Mr. S., however, kept up his visits, always unannounced, always near the closet and looking as he used to look, except for a certain fuzziness around the edges. He never said a word, though, and his widow wondered what on earth—or any place else—he wanted after all this time.

"Do you think there's something disturbing him?" I ventured, in German. But Mrs. S. missed the point.

"Right off the bat he disturbed me, that's what he did," she countered. "Why, my son sat on a chair and he even knocked on that."

But I explained my question again and finally she understood and smiled wryly.

"He was an oddball, he was," she finally said slowly. "Toward the end, well, we had a good marriage, but the last six months of our life together we didn't live together."

Aha! I thought. Remorse! Evidently the red-hot grandmama didn't get all she expected from Mr. S. and it troubled him still. Nothing like a good man letting an even better woman down. Nothing, however, indicated any unfinished business on his part. Mrs. S. lived on a decent pension and at least in that respect Mr. S. had taken good care of his wife.

"I've had lots of holy masses said for him," Mrs. S. explained. "I've told him not to worry about anything any longer, but he keeps bothering me."

"Why do you suppose he does this?"

"I think he was sorry he married me. After he came back from his brother's funeral, he started to act kind of funny. It had to do with his sister-in-law. I think he would have married her if we had not been married already."

Because she was afraid of the visitations of her late husband—and, incidentally, his attentions—she took in a boarder, a young man. She felt better with a man around the house, she explained.

"Attentions?" I asked.

"Yes," she nodded gravely and somewhat with embarrassment. "I felt him next to me in bed. I know it was him. I recognized his touch."

I explained that it looked to me as though her late husband had settled for her after all, and not the sister-in-law. Perhaps if she accepted his posthumous favors in the spirit in which they were given? I instructed her how to deal with Mr. S. next time he showed himself, to tell him, "I love you, yes, but please go away and don't bother me. And about those six months when you weren't much good—forget it, it was nice to have a rest. Above all, don't feel guilty."

She understood what the problem was now.

Was there any problem between them because of their different religions? She was Catholic and he was Protestant, and the holy masses had been Catholic masses.

"Oh, no," she replied, "it wouldn't have mattered to him. He didn't believe in anything."

There was a rustling in back of us. I had become so engrossed in my interview with the spunky eighty-four-year-old lady that I had completely forgotten about *Das Hamburg Fernsehen,* the Hamburg TV people, who had been filming the scene furiously. There remained only the actual exorcism ceremony to be done. I waited until the cameraman had changed magazines, then I instructed Mrs. S. to repeat after me, word for word, sentence for sentence.

"Adolph Paul S.," I began, "you are not to come here any longer."

"Any longer," Mrs. S. repeated.

"I have forgiven you, I love you, but the time has come for you to join your relatives."

"Join your relatives," intoned Mrs. S. I discovered an urgency I had not put into my own words. Perhaps the thought of sending him home to his relatives was particularly pleasing to her.

"Go in peace, and don't return here any more. The door is closed."

"Closed," repeated Mrs. S. and looked up at me. The television people started to pack their gear. Mrs. S. broke out some *Schnaps,* insisting we join her in a glass of the good stuff to celebrate the expected departure of her late husband to territories whence no train returns.

I smiled at her. She was full of life and her eyes sparkled. Eighty-four, I thought, my God, she's going to be around another fifty years.

"Even my boarder heard it," she said suddenly. We had forgotten about the boarder.

"What about him?" I questioned her.

Klaus W., a young man who worked in the market, had not only told her about his troubles with the ghost —he had also told his mother. Mother had come and talked about it with Mrs. S.

"Three times it happened," Mrs. S. said, "and each time I told him it was just the passing cars. After all, I didn't want to lose him."

But there were those strange, knocking noises in the middle of the night. In the end, Klaus couldn't take it any more. He moved out, but recommended a friend for the vacant room.

Either the husband doesn't like to talk to the new boarder or the new boarder sleeps more soundly than his predecessor, but so far there were no complaints.

Mrs. S. then insisted we should look at her kitchen cabinet where she had heard all the noises and where her husband had been "in residence."

"That's how he did it," she said sharply and rapped on the wood, "knocking, knocking, knocking!"

She was getting excited again and I reminded her that we had, after all, sent Mr. S. to his just rewards. I shook hands with Mrs. S., and we left. The television people weren't sure when the station would run the film. Fortunately they ran it after our departure from Hamburg. Had they shown it during my stay, there would have been considerable damage among TV executives. A friend of mine saw the resulting film. It was all very factual except for a small epilogue by a station spokesman questioning my honesty. The next time a Hamburg TV man wants an interview I will refer him to the nearest practitioner of black magic. For a treatment.

Two weeks later I had a letter from Mrs. S. It would seem that the press was bothering her since the TV film had been shown. In fact, it was worse than being bothered by her late husband. And speaking of the devil— her late husband—things weren't going well at all.

The knocking continued, and the prickling sensation she had so often felt when the dear departed one was hovering around was back again. Could I please come back and do it all over again? And bring a medium?

I felt genuinely sorry for the old lady and I explained what I had not had the courage to say before. That it was her continuing demands on an active life, and her unusual overabundance of that same life force, that kept supplying the energy for the phenomena.

XIII

A STRANGER IN
YOUR BED

I t is bad enough when someone you knew in life wants to continue a relationship beyond the grave, but at least you know who you're dealing with. But what about a case where the physical attention comes from someone you didn't even know when he was alive?

Marlene S. is a thirty-seven-year-old housewife who is neither given to explorations into the unknown nor particularly involved in anything out of the ordinary. After two years of college she found that family life took up most, if not all, of her time, but she is still hoping to get her teacher's degree, after which she would like to teach English literature on a secondary level. But with four youngsters—ranging in age from eleven to fifteen —and a husband around the house, time for study is limited. Her husband is a district manager for a shoe company.

Marlene came from an average Nebraska family and nothing particularly shocking ever happened to her, until she, her husband, and their children moved in

1958 into a house in Kansas City that will be forever etched in her memories. The house itself was nothing special: about seven years old, inexpensive-looking, with four bedrooms, built ranch-style all on one floor. A few weeks after they had settled down and gotten used to the new surroundings, Marlene was lying awake in bed, waiting to fall asleep. She never could go to sleep right away, and lying awake trying to sort things out in her mind was her way of inviting the sandman.

Because the children were still young, ranging in age from one to five, she had to be always alert for any moves or noises in case something was wrong. Perhaps this contributed to her light sleep, but at any rate she was not yet drowsy at this point and was fully cognizant of what might transpire around her.

Suddenly she felt pressure at the foot of the bed as if one of the children was trying to climb into bed to sleep with the parents. Marlene sat up quickly but quietly, leaned toward the foot of the bed, made a grab, at the same time saying, "Got you!"—only to find herself grabbing thin air.

She assumed the little culprit had quickly scuttled back to his own bed, and got up and went across the hall to the boys' bedroom. After that, she inspected the girls' room, but all four were sound asleep, tucked in precisely the way she had earlier tucked them in and it was clear that none of her children had caused the pressure at the foot of her bed.

She decided she had imagined the whole thing and went back to bed. But the following night, the pressure was back again and again she grabbed nothing but a fistful of thin air.

It got to be such a common occurrence she quit

checking on the children. She then decided that it had to be caused by her husband's moving his foot in a certain way. Somehow she reasoned that his moves gave the feeling the covers were drawn up against her foot, creating the impression of an outside pressure. Farfetched though this explanation was, she accepted it gladly. But she kept her foot against his for several nights after this to find out what move of his caused all this to happen.

As her husband slept, she observed, but it got her nowhere: the pressure was still present, but there was no connection with her husband's foot or his movements.

She had hardly accepted the strange pressure in her bed when still another phenomenon caused her to wonder about the house. Near the doorway to the bedroom she heard someone breathe deeply and heavily, but there was no one around. When this recurred several times she decided to tell her husband about it. He shook his head and said he had heard nothing. She did not tell him about the pressure on the bed, thinking it just too absurd to discuss. That night she heard the crackling of what sounded like someone stepping on cellophane just before she felt the pressure at the foot of the bed again.

She knew she had left a cellophane bag on the floor at the foot of the bed and she was sure one of her children had come out and stepped on it. Again she grabbed but again her hands held only air and the children were all soundly asleep in their respective rooms.

By now a little bit of fear crept into her mind when she came to realize that there wasn't really any rational explanation for the strange noises and especially for the heavy breathing. But she pulled her knees up at night and thus avoided coming in contact with whatever was causing the pressure at the foot of the bed.

For a while nothing untoward happened, and the family was busy getting on with the problems of daily living. The strange occurrences drifted into the background for a while. Then one night, several weeks later, Marlene was awakened from sleep by a most incredible sound. It was as if a giant vat of water was being poured on the house. The swooshing sound of water cascading down upon them reverberated for several seconds afterward. Her immediate thought, being just awakened from deep sleep, was a logical one—one of the kids had not been able to make it to the bathroom and what she was hearing was the result! But no: they were all fast asleep in their rooms.

The next morning, she examined the floor. In the boys' room she found a strange liquid spot. It was like water, except much thicker and did not ooze out as water would, but lay there on the floor, perfectly cohesive and round. It had neither odor nor color and when she removed it with tissue paper, it left no trace. Her husband explained that probably the liquid had oozed up from the ground or dropped from the ceiling but her logical mind refused to accept what was obviously not likely.

There was absolutely no rational explanation for either the swooshing noise or the presence of the thick liquid in the boys' room. Several months afterward, a similar spot appeared in the girls' room. Since they had no animals in the house, the matter remained a puzzle.

The house was so new that any thoughts of ghosts were furthest from Marlene's mind. But other strange things occurred. One day a car securely parked across from the house on a slanting driveway came downhill and crashed into the boys' bedroom. Luckily no one was hurt. Not much later, another car from across the street did the same thing, only this time the car went into the girls' room. The owner swore he had put the car into parking position on leaving it. Just as he got out, he saw his car roll down the driveway by *itself!*

This wasn't too reassuring to Marlene. Was some unknown force trying to "get" them? Was there a connection between the spots of liquid in the childrens' bedrooms and the two car crashes?

Somehow the atmosphere in the house was different now from the time they had first moved in. It seemed heavy, as if some sort of tragic pressure was weighing upon it. Her husband did not notice anything unusual, or if he did, he did not discuss it with her. But to her there was an ominous presence in the house and she didn't like it.

One night her husband was working late. She had gone to bed and had just turned the lights out when she began to hear the heavy breathing again. Next came the pressure at the foot of the bed. With the breathing so close to her, she was absolutely terrified and dared not move. Whatever it was, it was very near and she realized now that all her reasoning had not explained a thing. *Someone other than herself shared her bed and that someone was not friendly.*

But what was she to do? The children were asleep in their beds and her husband was at work. She decided that under the circumstances the best thing was to play possum. She lay there as if asleep, barely breathing and not moving a muscle.

She did not know how much time had passed when

she heard the car drive up to their door. The headlights shone through the bedroom window and she heard the motor being turned off.

"Thank God, Don is home," she managed to say under her breath.

Even though the presence was still close by, she somehow managed to get enough courage to jump out of bed and race to the window. Turning on the lights on the way to the living room as she went by, she reached the window and looked out to the driveway.

Instead of seeing her husband and the family car, she was greeted by the blackness of the night. Nothing. No car.

"This is the last straw!" she almost cried and ran back to her bed. Pulling the covers over her she lay there in terror, not knowing what to do next. When her husband finally returned after what seemed hours upon hours, she managed to sob out her story.

"There, there," he said, soothingly, taking her head in his hands. "You've been having nightmares."

"He doesn't believe a word I've said," she thought between sobs, but she preferred being consoled by a nonbeliever than not being consoled at all.

The next few weeks passed somehow. They had requested a transfer to another location. When it came, she was a new person. The prospect of moving into another house where nothing would disturb her sleep was just too wonderful.

Her husband had rented a big, old mansion in Wichita, where they were transferred by the company, and it was filled with antiques and fine furniture of a bygone era. When Marlene first saw the house, she thought, "Oh my God, if any house ought to be haunted, this looks like one!" But it wasn't and the house in Wichita proved as peaceful and serene as a house can be, if it isn't inhabited by a restless ghost.

The house was full of memories of its past fifty years but none of them intruded upon her and she lived a happy, relaxed life now. The experiences in Kansas receded into her memory and she was sure now that it had all been the fault of the house and not something connected with her—least of all, her imagination, for she knew, no matter what her husband had said, that she had seen and heard that ghost car drive up to the house.

She sometimes wonders who the new owners of that house in Kansas are and whether they can hear the heavy breathing the way she did. But then she realizes that it was her own innate psychic ability that allowed the phenomena to manifest themselves when they did. Another person not so endowed might conceivably not feel anything at all.

What was the horrible accident that was being reenacted—from the sound of the water being poured down, to the rushing up of the ghost car? And whose heavy breathing was disturbing her nights?

Many times her curiosity almost made her inquire but then she decided to let sleeping dogs lie. But in later years while living in California, her psychic ability developed further until she was able to hear and see the dead as clearly and casually as she could commune with the living. It frightened her and she thought at first she was having waking nightmares. All through the night she would be aware of a room full of people while at the same time being able to sleep on. Her observation was on several levels at the same time, as if she had been turned into a radio receiver with several bands.

Clearly she did not want any of this, least of all the heavy breathing she started to hear again after they had moved to California. But then it could be the breathing of another restless soul, she decided, and not necessarily something or someone she had brought with her from Kansas.

She read as much as she could on the subject of ESP, and tried her hand at automatic writing. To her surprise, her late father and her grandparents wrote to her through her. She noticed that the various messages were in different hands and quite clearly differed from her own. Yet her logical mind told her this might all come from her own subconscious mind and she began to reject it. As she closed herself off from the messages, they dwindled away until she no longer received them.

This she regretted, for the presence of her father to continue the link of a lifetime and perhaps protect her from the incursions of unwanted entities of both worlds was welcome and reassuring.

By now she knew of her psychic powers and had learned to live with them, but also to close the psychic door when necessary.

Meanwhile the house in Kansas still stands, and very few tenants stay for long.

A GHOSTLY SEDUCTION

Though the majority of physical encounters between a discarnate and a living person may not be exactly welcome, that is not to say that such relationships are just a product of the fertile imagination of the living partner. Then, too, there are some cases where the incursion from Beyond is not exactly sought, but is quietly encouraged through prayer, meditation, and strong feelings of loneliness and a desire to have the physical relationship somehow continue.

But what I am about to report is none of the above. The parties involved did not know each other, or of each other, until they shared the same physical space. I thought I had "laid to rest" a certain young lady ghost in a Brooklyn College residence, but lo and behold, the story was apparently not quite finished. Some time after my initial investigation, when I followed up on a report by four girls who lived in a flat in that house, I was contacted by some male students in great excitement. "Henny," as they had come to call the ghost, was apparently still active, and would I please do something about it.

Henny used to live in one of those old brownstone houses in a better section of Brooklyn. The house had been turned into a boarding house for students and professional people. Henny worked in a department store, having been unable to finish college. But she always had a great admiration for those who did, and dated many students and even teachers over the years. Dated is perhaps the wrong term, because Henny had both an extremely good figure and an insatiable appetite for sex. Unfortunately she also had a heart defect and passed away in her thirties. What had been her room at the boarding house was used by many others as time went on.

I don't know whether people had problems with her ghost until I heard about it, but a couple of Brooklyn College students called me in great excitement when Henny appeared to them. George, one of the two young fellows, had gone to bed in his room in that house—still a rooming house today—when he was awakened in the small of the night by a strange glow emanating from the ceiling. He checked it out and found no source for it, but decided to blame it on passing cars. He had hardly laid down again when the glow became brighter and turned into the pulsating figure of a young woman dressed in clothes of another era.

George sat up in bed and watched dumbfounded as the woman came toward him and began to stroke his head. He actually felt her caress, which seemed very cold and clammy when her hands touched his forehead. But there was nothing there. Being only half awake, George somehow thought that she was one of the girls from the upper floors, but he really didn't mind, especially as the girl also took off her blouse and pressed her breasts against his chest. He could not help observing that her breasts were enormous and that her lips, touching his, were cold as ice. George does not remember any more than this; when he awoke the next day he thought it had all been a sexy dream. He made light of it to his landlady, who was not at all amused by his graphic description of the girl's assets. "You wait here a moment," she finally demanded and rushed off to her own apartment. When she returned a moment later, she held a yellowed newspaper clipping in her hand. "Does that look anything like the woman you saw in your dream?" George took a look at the clipping. "Why, it *is* her," he replied. The clipping was the girl's obituary from over twenty years ago!

Since I had been asked to do something about poor Henny, I returned a week later with a good trance medium, Ethel Johnson Meyers, and we contacted Henny. The contact broke her obsession with the living and she left, somewhat tearfully but in peace.

XV

THE AFFAIR DEATH COULD NOT STOP

Keep in mind that "ghosts" are really people who have passed from the physical world into the next world but are still fully conscious of their personalities and desires, though now residing, as it were, in a "lighter" body, solid to themselves but invisible to most flesh-and-blood people, though not necessarily to someone with whom they have a strong and lasting emotional bond.

This is not the norm of passing, of course, but rather the exception, and prevents the discarnate person from truly going on into the next stage of existence and eventually reincarnating again. But that is rarely on the mind of someone who regrets having left the body with much unfinished business of various kinds. The case I am about to report is extraordinary, but I am firmly convinced that it did occur as told.

Mrs. S. is the controller of a large art school in one of the Western states, but before she obtained this rather important position in her town she had many other jobs. Among them was an executive secretarial position for a manufacturing concern. At the time she worked there, a certain Mr. M. was the company's manager. The very first day they met there was a strong bond between them. If ever there was love at first sight, this was an example of it. He never told her that he loved her, and they did not get married, but she knew how he felt about her nevertheless. M. was an extremely active executive who liked to do things himself, attend conferences, run things, be behind the manipulations and intrigues of a large corporation. He was at the top when Mrs. S. knew him, and he was a busy man, so that whatever time they could spend together was precious minutes. In the 1960s he became chairman of the board and no longer took an active interest in the operations of the company. Instead his fertile mind directed itself toward new business ventures, investments, real estate, and, particularly, the aviation industry. He himself held a pilot's license and flew several planes. In May 1971 he lost his life in a seaplane accident in the Columbia River. It was an unusually stormy day; the waves were four feet high. He landed all right in a small cove, but when he tried to take off again, the plane flipped over. He and his passenger held onto the plane for several hours before attempting to swim to shore. Unfortunately the undertow was too strong, and M. didn't make it.

That very night Mrs. S. had a dream that he was with her. She saw him standing beside her, and after he had caressed her, she heard him say, "I didn't make it." She awoke from this vivid dream, not understanding what it all meant. The early morning radio news told her.

For about ten or twelve days she went around in a daze, totally destroyed by the separation. Then something strange happened. She was having conversations with Mr. M. At first she rejected the notion, having had no previous knowledge of anything psychic in her life. She thought, quite naturally, that it was her own unconscious giving her a bad time due to the shock of his sudden passing. But the conversations became more pronounced and the messages more urgent. Material was brought to her consciousness she was not aware of. Gradually she became convinced that it was indeed Mr. M. conversing with her, and she responded accordingly. Just as he had in his life, he commanded her now. She heard him say that her job at the museum wasn't as important as going to another city. She didn't want to go there and argued with him. He insisted. Several days later, while she was in the middle of fixing supper, she heard him say to her that the supper could wait, that she must go now to the library. So she went to the library, and there she found some books on ESP and parapsychology. That is how she came to me, and how her report on the extraordinary events in her life followed. Just as he had requested, she drove to that nearby city. Mr. M. was with her all the time.

They arrived there early in the morning when there was hardly anyone around. He insisted they go up to what was his house. A sign said KEEP OUT. Mrs. S. stopped and looked over the wall. Apparently someone was still taking care of the house, for everything seemed in good order. She heard Mr. M. ask her, "Do you think you would be happy here?" "Not without you," she heard herself reply. He seemed to laugh at this notion. "Who says without me." "Well, but how?" "I'll be with you." "But how could I live here? The gates are locked."

"You'll see." With a twist of illogical and yet perfectly natural thinking, she complained, "But you never even told me that you loved me." "What more can a man say? How much more should I do to show you that I love you?" "You never married me." "I never married anyone else either."

He then went on to explain that he wanted her to carry on his business so that the people who had worked under him would understand what he had wanted done. In view of the magnitude of his enterprises, she was shocked. He took it for hesitation and asked, "Do you have any reservations?" Then she understood why he had told her earlier that her job at the museum wasn't nearly as important as that which he had in mind for her. He explained that she knew enough about finances that she could manage a company such as his and assured her that everything had been carefully planned by him.

Several weeks went by. Evidently Mr. M. had problems adjusting to the afterlife, but he managed it, and the communications continued. "Somehow he can be part of me," Mrs. S. explained, "I don't understand at all how, but he is. He comes and goes. When he's with me, he's on my left side from my shoulder and neck and arm down to my waist. He covers about half of me, and he weighs something but not very much. For about a week at first, it was a throbbing, painful, and burning feeling, but the pain diminished," she said. All this was new and startling to her. She neither invited nor resisted it, but she was overawed at the thought that Mr. M. would use her as the vehicle of his further expansion from the world beyond. A week later he woke her in the middle of the night just to say he loved her. Finally she heard him say those words she had waited for all those years. Then a couple of days later he returned. It was three o'clock in the morning and she awoke but couldn't move at all. She felt a number of persons around her including Mr. M., although she could not say a word. Then all of a sudden she felt herself pulled from above and out of her body, and she saw a dazzling, beautiful white light just beyond where she was. A moment later she was dropped back into her bed and could move again. She woke up exhausted and wringing wet. Not sure what all this meant and what might happen next, she decided to make out her will.

It was now early July 1971, and Mr. M. had become part and parcel of Mrs. S.'s daily activities. He even went shopping with her and expressed definite likes and dislikes. To her, it was fun having someone along whom no one else could see, and sharing things with him. Of course she had to watch herself when she wanted to talk out loud. It was easy to be taken for insane in this straight and narrow world. One day while she was sitting on her patio taking the sun, she asked, "What interests you?" "Making love," he replied and proceeded to do it. "I don't know exactly how he does it," Mrs. S. confided, "but it is very enjoyable. I hope so for him too." Afterward he said, "You are very beautiful." Under the circumstances she felt herself married and said so much to him and how happy she was, adding that she would like to have a ring. He promised to do something about it. "One with our birthstones," she added. It didn't occur to her that there was something strange about asking a discarnate person to furnish her with a

wedding ring. Anyone who would continue a conversation or make love to her the way Mr. M. had done a
considerable time after his earthly demise should be able
to provide a ring too.

XVI

THE GHOSTLY
BEDMATE

My friend says this skeleton tried to get into bed with her," my friend Elizabeth Byrd said with conviction and looked at me straight to see how I would react. I did not disappoint her. I shook my head with determination and informed her somewhat haughtily that skeletons do not get into people's beds, in fact skeletons don't do much really except maybe on Halloween when there's kids inside them.

But Elizabeth is as good a researcher as she is an author—*Immortal Queen* and *Flowers of the Forest* are among her historical novels—and she insisted that this was not some sort of Halloween prank.

More to please her than out of curiosity, I decided to look into this weird tale. I never take stock in anything that I don't hear firsthand, so I called on Elizabeth's friend to hear all about this skeleton myself. I was prepared for a charming, garrulous spinster whose imagination was running away with her.

The name on the door read Dianne Nicholson, and it was one of those grimy walk-ups on New York's middle East Side that are slowly but surely turning into slums. Downstairs there was a gun shop and the house was squeezed in between a row of other nondescript houses. Children, none of them particularly tidy-looking, were playing in the street, and trucks lumbered by me on Second Avenue creating a steady din that must have been unnerving to any resident of this building.

I pressed the bell and when the buzzer responded, I walked up a flight of stairs, where I found the entrance door to the apartment in the front part of the building slightly ajar. I stepped inside and closed the door behind me.

"Miss Nicholson?" I said tentatively.

"Coming," a bell-like young voice came from the back of the dimly lit apartment.

As my eyes got used to the place I distinguished that it consisted of a longish foyer from which doors led to a kitchen, another room, and a small room, reading right to left. It was a jumble of furniture and things and a glance into the small room on my left showed stacks of papers, a drawing board, and other graphic art paraphernalia strewn about.

My investigation was interrupted by the arrival of Miss Nicholson. It was immediately clear that my image of her had been wrong. An ash blonde of perhaps twenty-two or twenty-three, she was slight and erect and looked very determined as she greeted me from the other room in center.

"I'm so glad you came," she began and led me to the couch along the wall of the foyer. "This thing has been getting out of hand lately."

I held up my hand—for I did not want to lose a

word of her account. Within a minute, my tape recorder was purring away and the story unfolded.

Dianne Nicholson came to New York from her native Atlanta in the middle of 1964. By training she was a writer, or more specifically, a writer of publicity, advertising, and promotional material, and she was presently working with an advertising agency in Manhattan. She was much too busy with the task of looking for a job and then of maintaining it to pay much attention to the house and the little apartment in it that she had rented. It was inexpensive and within her budget, she did not have to share it with a roommate, and that was what she had wanted. If it was no luxury building, well, it was also convenient to her place of work and she had no complaints.

In addition, she did a lot of extra work at home, free-lance accounts to better her income, so she was rather absorbed in her professional activities most of the time, seldom allowing herself the luxury of aimless dreaming. Her social life was pleasant, but underneath it all ran a very practical streak, for Dianne had come to New York to make a successful career for herself.

She knew few if any of her neighbors, most of whom were not in her social or professional strata to begin with. But she did manage to strike up a friendship with the girl who had an apartment a few stories above hers. This was a German girl in her early thirties who went by the single name of Karina. An artist specializing in small drawings and cards, Karina went around her place most of the time wearing miniskirts even before miniskirts had come into fashion. Her life was lived mainly on the inside of herself and she was happy to pursue this kind of career. Evidently she had left behind her in Germany a far different life, but there were no regrets. The two girls visited each other frequently, and it made both of them feel safe to know neither was entirely alone in this dank building.

It was in the middle of 1965, after living in the building for about a year, that Dianne became alarmed by a sequence of events she could not cope with. At the time she slept in the smaller room, off the foyer, which later became her workroom.

She awoke there one night and saw a figure standing at her door. It was a rather tall woman, wearing what to Dianne looked like a long nightgown. The figure also wore a kind of Mother Hubbard cap, like a granny would—and yet Dianne quickly realized that this was not an old figure at all.

As Dianne—at first with curiosity and then with increasing terror—sat up in bed and studied the apparition, she noticed that the figure was luminescent and emitted a soft, white glow. The face, or rather the area where the facial characteristics should be, was also aglow, but she could not make out any features. As yet unsure as to what the figure was, Dianne noticed she could not distinguish any hands either.

At this moment the figure left the spot at the door and got into bed with her. When the figure got close Dianne's first impression was that of a skeleton, but when it got into bed with her she realized that it was more of a waxen figure, very cold but as hard as flesh would be.

Her mind racing while her body was practically paralyzed, Dianne tried to reason it out. Then she said to herself, why, it must be my mother. What in the world would come into bed with her?

Later she realized that it wasn't her mother, of course. But at the moment she preferred to think so, recalling how her mother had often crawled into bed with her when she was a child. And yet she knew at this moment, crystal clear, that the white figure next to her was that of a young woman.

Touching the figure, she felt hard substance underneath the gown.

"I must see your face," she mumbled and tried to see the stranger's face. But the figure acted as if she were asleep and did not wish to be disturbed.

Dianne reached out and pulled the covers off the bed. She found herself staring into a mirror. Now she realized why she had not been able to see the creature's hands before. They weren't really hands at all, but were more like a skeleton's bony fingers, holding up a mirror in front of the figure's face.

Then the mirror moved and disclosed what took the place of a face: a glowing white round in which neither eyes, nose, nor teeth could be distinguished and yet the whole figure was more than a mere anatomical skeleton—it was a roughly covered skeleton figure—more than mere bones and not quite flesh and skin, but somewhere in between.

Dianne's normal reactions finally caught up with her; she found herself sinking into a slow state of shock at what she had discovered. At this moment, the figure disappeared. Not by retreating to the doorway from where it had come, but just by dissolving from the bed itself.

Dianne leaped out of bed, threw on a robe, and raced upstairs to her friend's apartment. For days after, she trembled at the thought of the unspeakable one returning, and she tried hard to convince herself that she had dreamed the whole incident. But in her heart she knew she had not.

From that day on, however, she became increasingly aware of a human presence other than her own in the apartment. More from self-preservation through knowledge than from idle curiosity, she bought some books dealing with psychic phenomena.

Early in December this oppressive feeling became suddenly very strong. Dianne had moved her bed into the other bedroom, with a wall separating the two areas. One night she *knew* that an attack had been made upon her and that the evil personality involved was male. She slept with all the lights on from that moment. With mounting terror she would not go off to sleep until daylight reassured her that no further dangers were about.

Then in early January 1966, just before I came to see her, Dianne had another visit from a white, luminous figure. It was evening, and Dianne had just gotten to sleep. Suddenly she awoke, prodded by some inborn warning system, and there in the entrance to her present bedroom stood a vague, smokelike figure of some luminescence. After a moment it was gone, only to return again later that same night. Dianne was not alone that night, but it did not help her fears. What did the figure want of her? This was not the skeletal visitor from before but a definitely masculine personality. Dianne knew this entity was after her, and wanted to take her over. On one occasion in December she had felt him take over her nervous system, as she sat helplessly on her bed. Her muscles went into spasms as if they were no longer under her conscious control. Desperately she fought the invader, trying to keep her thoughts on an even keel, and ultimately she won out. The strange feeling left her body and she was able to relax at last.

Extrasensory experiences had plagued Dianne since childhood. When she was fourteen and going to high school, a close friend and sorority sister wrote to her with a strange request. Would she sing at her funeral? Now Dianne had been singing in choir and her friend knew this. But there was no logical reason for so strange a request from a fifteen-year-old girl. Three days after receiving the letter Dianne had a strange dream, in which she saw her friend in front of a large crowd, with her arms wide open, and calling out to Dianne, "Please help me!"

At this point, the dream faded out. She woke up after the dream and noticed that the clock showed 12:45 A.M., Friday. Sunday night, the identical dream returned, only this time it ended abruptly rather than gently fading out. She discussed the dreams with her classmates in school but could not puzzle out the meaning. On Tuesday she received a phone call from her mother, informing her that her friend had been in an automobile accident on Friday, and at the time of Dianne's first dream the friend had just gone under the anaesthetic at the hospital. At the time of the second dream, which ended abruptly, the girl died.

There were other instances of premonitions come true, of feelings about events that later transpired—making Dianne aware of the fact that she had something special, yet in no way intruding on her practical approach to life.

When she first moved into her present apartment, she found that most of the buildings in the area were occupied by people on welfare relief. But the house she moved into had recently been renovated, making it suitable for higher-rent tenants, as had two others nearby, giving hope that the entire neighborhood might eventually adopt a different image.

Although one of Dianne's boyfriends, a photographer, felt nothing special about the apartment, two of her female friends did. There was Karina, the artist upstairs, for instance. She would not stay long, complaining the place gave her the creeps. Elizabeth Byrd also felt an oppressiveness not borne out by the decor or furniture of the place, for Dianne had managed to make the place comfortable and pleasant as far as the purely physical aspects were concerned.

After a while she quit her Madison Avenue job and became free-lance. This necessitated her spending much more time at home. In the daytime she found the place peaceful and quiet and she managed to get her work done without trouble. But as soon as the shadows of night crept over the horizon, fear began to return to her heart. The fear was not borne from darkness or from the presence of the unknown; it was almost a physical thing with her, something very tangible that seemed to fill a space within the walls of her apartment.

Dianne thought herself safe from the specter in the daytime until one morning she was awakened by a strange noise. She had gone to bed late after putting in long hours of work, and slept until 10 A.M. The noise, she soon realized, was caused by a wooden coat hanger banging heavily against the bedroom door. Still half-asleep, Dianne assured herself that the draft was causing it. She got out of bed, fully awake now, and walked toward the door. The noise stopped abruptly. She checked the door and windows and found everything closed. There could not have been a draft. Still unconvinced, she huffed and puffed to see if her breath would move the hanger. It didn't.

She began to have some strange dreams, several similar ones in succession. In these dreams the skeleton-faced white woman appeared to her and wanted to take her with her.

As the weeks rolled by, more and more strange incidents tried her patience sorely. There was the time she had gone to sleep with all lights burning, when she saw an explosion of light in the living room. It was not hallucinatory, for she saw it reflected in the dark screen of her television set. Another time she was in the bedroom when she heard the sound of glass breaking in the living room. The lights in the living room and the kitchen went out at the same moment. She entered the living room, expecting to see the remnants of a bulb that might have blown up, but there was nothing on the floor. The light switches in both living room and kitchen, however, had been switched off by unseen hands. . . . At this moment her friend Karina came down from upstairs and Dianne was never so glad in her life to see a friendly human face.

Since Dianne Nicholson had gotten to be quite frantic about all this I decided to arrange for a seance to get to the bottom of the disturbances with the help of a good medium. We agreed on June 17, 1966, as the date, Sybil Leek was to be my medium, and Theo Wilson, a reporter from the *Daily News,* would come along to witness and report on the investigation.

Meanwhile, Karina had also had her share of run-ins with the Uninvited. Her apartment is on the fifth floor. One day Karina was standing in front of her mirror when she noticed a ghostly figure—or rather a glowing outline. At the same time she felt a strong urge to cut her hair short and be like the apparition. She felt the ghostly presence wanted to possess her or express itself through her and she became frightened. A little later she was down on the second floor with Dianne when both girls heard a sharp banging noise, as if someone had dumped a heavy object on the floor next to the entrance of the apartment. Their first impression was that a package had been delivered and they rushed to see what it was. But there was nothing there.

When the seventeenth of June arrived it turned out to be one of those oppressive, prematurely hot New York nights, but the date had been set and everyone was in readiness. I also brought along a motion picture camera and on arrival had deposited Sybil with Karina so that I might discuss the events leading up to the investigation once more for the benefit of Theo Wilson of the *News*. Naturally Sybil was not to hear any of this nor was Karina allowed to discuss anything with her temporary guest but the weather—at the moment a most timely subject.

Half an hour later I brought Sybil inside the second floor apartment. Did she feel anything here clairvoyantly?

"You'll probably laugh at this," Sybil said, "but I have a tremendous feeling about horses."

I didn't laugh, and even though I knew of Sybil's love for and interest in domestic animals, I noted the statement for later verification.

"What about people, though?" I pressed. A heavy oak chair had been placed near the entrance to the smaller room where Dianne had experienced the skeletal intruder originally. The chair was meant for Sybil to sit in and faced away from the small room.

"Behind this chair," Sybil now said, "there is a touch of coldness . . . some nonphysical being, definitely."

The feeling was only fleeting, her main sensation being of a country place with horses, and then that touch of "someone."

I decided to place Sybil into trance now and we— our hostess Dianne Nicholson, a gentleman friend of hers, Karina, Theo Wilson, and myself—grouped ourselves around her. Sybil took the chair facing away from the little room.

After a few moments, heavy, labored breathing replaced the measured breath of Sybil's normal personality. Words came across her lips that I could not yet make out, gradually becoming louder and firmer. I kept asking for a name—asking that the presence identify itself. Eventually the name was clear.

"Jeremy Waters," Sybil had said.

"Speak louder," I commanded.

"Go away," the voice countered, and added, "Jeremy."

"Why should Jeremy go away?"

"Why did he do it . . . nice stock . . . I'm hurt . . . Jeremy, Jeremy Waters . . ."

"Who are you?"

"Waters."

"Who is Jeremy?"

"Jeremy Waters, my son . . . I'll find him . . . ran away . . . left me . . . what'd he leave me for? . . . Mary Collins . . ."

It dawned on me now that Jeremy Waters, Sr., was complaining about Jeremy Waters, Jr.

"Is this your house?" I asked.

"House? There is not a house," the voice came back, somewhat astonished.

"Store place . . . I work here . . . waiting for Jeremy . . . where did they go, Jeremy and Marie . . . his woman . . ."

"How long ago was this?"

"Strange . . . fifty-four . . . where's everyone?"

"Tell me about yourself so I can help you."

"I don't trust you. What have you done with him?"

"What sort of work does he do?"

"A boat. He brings things here."

"When were you born?"

"Twenty-two."

"Where?"

"Hudson village . . ."

"What is your wife's name?"

"Margie."

"Where was she born?"

"Far . . . in Holland."

"Any children?"

"Jeremy . . . three."

When I asked what church he belonged to I got a disdainful snort in reply.

"Churches . . . churches . . . I do not go."

"What sort of place is this?"

"What do you come here for? Fall on your knees . . ." he said, instead, and added, "Find Jeremy . . . he should repent his sins . . . honor thy father and thy mother . . . where am I? There are too many people. . . ." The voice sounded confused and worried now.

"And where's his clothes?" he demanded to know.

I started to explain the passage of time.

"Repent, repent," he mumbled instead, barely listening.

"Why did they do it? Hurt me?"

"Who is this woman you mentioned?"

"Maria Goulando." It had sounded like Mary Collins to me at first, but now there was no mistaking the odd name. "She is Jeremy's woman."

"Is he married to her?"

"It is wrong to marry a Catholic," the voice said sternly.

"Is the girl a Catholic?"

"Yes."

"Did he marry her?"

"Over my dead body."

"He didn't marry her then?"

"No . . . the church won."

"Where is the woman now?"

"With Jeremy."

"If you find them, what will you do?"

"Make him repent."

This was said with so much bitterness I decided to take another tack with my questioning. "Have you hurt anyone, Jeremy?" I said.

"Why are you asking me . . . I'm not going to talk," he shot back, defiant again.

"Do you know where you are?"

"Outside the church."

"What church?"

"Lutheran church."

"Are you a Lutheran then?"

"Was . . ."

"What are you now?"

"*Nothing* . . ."

"What street is the church on?"

"Vall Street."

If he meant to say Wall Street he said it with a strange inflection.

I asked him to spell it.

Puzzled and haltingly he said, "Veh—ah—el—el," spelling the W the way a European might spell it, especially a Dutchman or German.

"Wall Street," the voice said more clearly now, this time pronouncing it correctly.

"Name of the church?" I inquired.

"Why—can't—I—find—him?" it came back haltingly.

"What is this place used for?"

"Store things in the back . . ."

"Where do you live?"

"Hudson . . . up the Hudson."

Again I asked for the year he thought we were in.

"Fifty-four . . ."

This is where I made a mistake, perhaps.

"Eighteen fifty-four?" I said. I never like to lead.

"Yes," the voice acknowledged and added, "February . . . today the fifteenth . . ."

"How old are you?" I asked.

"Today is my birthday."

"And your son is not with you?"

"Yes . . . ingratitude shall be his ruin."

"Did you kill anyone?"

"Go away, go away . . ." The voice sounded angry

now as if I had hit on a sensitive topic. I reasoned with him, explaining about the passage of time.

"Your son has long died," I explained.

He would not accept this.

"You're a foreigner," he suddenly said, "what do you want? *She's* a foreigner."

"You don't like foreigners?"

"No."

"Did you kill Maria?"

"She was a foreigner," he said with contempt in his voice.

I asked him to make a clean breast of his guilt feelings so that he might free himself from the place we had found him. There was a long, long pause. Finally he understood and listened quietly as I sent him away to rejoin his dead son. Soon after, I recalled Sybil to her own body. None the worse for her experience, she remembered absolutely nothing that had transpired during the seance.

So there were two ghosts, Jeremy Waters and the girl Maria.

My next step was to check out the names given and see how they connected with the place we were in.

Naturally I assumed that 1854 was the period I should check, since the ghost had acknowledged that date. But there was nothing in the records indicating a Jeremy Waters at that date living on 21st Street.

The only clue of some interest was the name of one James Waters, a "carman" who lived on East 22nd Street between Second and Third Avenues as of 1847, according to Doggett's *New York Directory* for that year. But the thought did not leave me that the "18" was added to the ghost's "54" by my suggestion. Could he have meant 1754?

I decided to check that earlier date. Suddenly things became more interesting.

The entire piece of land on which this and other houses in the block were standing had originally belonged to the Watts family. The Watts city residence stood at 59 East Twenty-first Street and John Watts, Sr., owned the land in 1754, together with his son, John Watts, Jr. I was struck by the similarity of names of father and son, a parallel to Jeremy, Sr., and Jeremy, Jr. They had acquired the land in 1747 from James De Lancey, the elder Watts's brother-in-law. It was then a farm of 130 acres. Spooner's *Historical Families in America,* which gives these and other details of the prominent Watts family, also states briefly that a third John Watts was born to the young John in 1775, but died unmarried.

I was still struggling with the research on this case when Theo Wilson's piece of our seance appeared in the New York *Daily News.* Theo was impressed by the sincerity of both approach and method and reported the investigation factually.

Because of her article a gentleman named Charles Burhaus contacted me with additional information on the Watts family; his father's sister had been married to the last of the Wattses. The Wattses did indeed come from the Hudson Valley and most of them are buried at Tivoli, New York.

The Wattses were very religious and fervent Protestants. "Old John" Watts, Mr. Burhaus reports, "disapproved of his son's way of living." When Mr. Burhaus's grandmother invited his Aunt Minnie to stay at the ancestral Watts house in Tivoli—Mr. Burhaus was then but a child—the lady refused to stay, explaining that the house was haunted by a ghost who liked women.

If there was a storehouse with boats nearby, as the ghost had claimed, on what is now East Twenty-first Street, 1854 would not fit, but 1754 would.

Jeremy Waters and John Watts are not identical names but I have encountered ghost personalities who, for reasons of honor, have disguised their true identities until the skill of the investigator was able to uncover their cover.

So much of the Waters father-and-son relationship seems to fit the Watts father-and-son relationship, the place is correct, and the first names are identical for father and son in both instances, that I cannot help feeling that we have this kind of situation here. If the son ran away with an unacceptable woman, the father would naturally not wish to divulge to a stranger, like me, his true identity, yet he might talk about the events themselves, being emotionally bound to them still.

Miss Nicholson had no further troubles in the apartment after that. She moved a few weeks later and the new occupants, if they know of my investigation at all, have not seen fit to complain about any disturbances.

So I can only assume that both Jeremy Waters, Sr., and the hapless girl he hurt have found their way across the boundary of the spirit world, which in any event is much nicer than a rooming house on East Twenty-first Street.

One more item gave me food for thought. I had taken a number of still photographs during the two visits to the apartment. When they were developed, several of them showed white shadows and streaks of light that could not be accounted for by natural explanations.

I mailed a set to Dianne Nicholson via first-class mail. It never reached her. About the same time, a letter containing some data on the apartment and its past, which she had mailed to me, never reached me. When I brought the negatives of my pictures to have another set of enlargements made, the lab could not account for the negatives, no reason given for the apparent loss.

Finally we had to rephotograph the only existing set of prints to make duplicates.

Coincidence? Perhaps.

If there is such a thing.

XVII

ELVIS PRESLEY AND THE WOMAN FROM A FORMER LIFE

In this day and age, when Elvis imitators are showing up all over, when fanatical fans report "seeing" Elvis alive and well, or living under an assumed name somewhere, I must report that the evidence for his passing when he did is indeed overwhelming. As is his "survival."

He is not hiding somewhere in obscurity (as some claim), not confiding his anguish to this or that publicity-seeking psychic reader, not a victim of suicide. Elvis lives, not just in our memories but in another dimension from which he has communicated with me and my associates. He has given overwhelming proof of his identity, and he has given us a message for the world he left.

"I am whole, I am well, I am here!" With those shattering words Elvis Presley's spirit reached across the gulf that separates his world from ours to communicate with his former bodyguard and stepbrother David Stanley and Stanley's mother, Dee Presley, in a spine-tingling two-hour seance arranged by me just a few days short of a year after the King of Rock died in his Memphis, Tennessee, home.

As the startled relatives looked on, wondering whether this was truly a contact, Elvis's spirit spoke with uncanny accuracy about intimate conversations the family had had before his death, secrets they had known but not publicized, places they had been together and experiences they had shared.

"I talked to Elvis, it was unbelievable," declared a shaken David Stanley, the thirty-three-year-old intimate of the King who came of age touring on the road with him. Stanley was at Graceland, Elvis's home, the day the star passed on. "The medium used the exact words Elvis told me two days before he died—*I'll be around,* I'll take care of you.' As a demonstration of psychic ability, the seance was authentic. It impressed me." To which Dee Presley added, "Oh yes, he was here, I know. It was a definite psychic contact."

But this dramatic confrontation was only the climax of several months of communications with Elvis Presley conducted in the privacy of my study through a timid, soft-spoken woman named Dorothy Sherry.

It is my profession to investigate unusual claims in parapsychology and sift the genuine from the false or doubtful, but three months of investigation and the most painstaking tests have now convinced me that Elvis Presley has indeed been in continual contact with Dorothy Sherry, whose role as the psychic go-between was neither chosen nor desired, and was in fact an accute source of embarrassment and fear for her at first until she began to work with me and to understand what was taking place.

Dorothy Sherry never met Elvis Presley, she had

not been to any concerts of his, does not collect his records or consider herself a fan of any kind. I've talked to a friend of hers and to her mother and verified these circumstances. But because the Presley communication came to her spontaneously, as a surprise and in a sense unwanted (though she has since accepted it), I consider Dorothy's case one of the most evidential instances of spirit communication in my many years as a practicing parapsychologist and researcher.

I also know why Presley picked this unlikely intermediary to be his spokeswoman in the world of flesh: her very lack of interest in his career and fame, her status as a simple housewife horrified by any thought of publicity or public acclaim, was ideally suited to make his attempt to communicate the more believable and the evidence therefore that much stronger.

At first I was extremely doubtful about the whole matter, as any scientific investigator is bound to be, especially when dealing with a well-known personality about whom much has been printed, published, and broadcast. Although I haven't the slightest doubt that Dorothy never read any books about Presley nor any newspaper stories concerning him, the fact that these sources exist must be taken into account when evaluating the evidence obtained through her entranced lips. But so many intimate details of Elvis's life unknown to the public at large have come to light in the course of my investigation that I cannot possibly doubt the authenticity of this contact from Beyond. Hours of in-depth investigative interviews, actual trance experiments, and other professional tests haven proven to me time and again, just as the final seance convinced the family, that

Elvis Presley is still very much able to communicate with our world.

With breathtaking accuracy Elvis revealed aspects of his life and family, his home and personality, that are simply too rich in detail and possessed of the human mood and flavor of Elvis to be derived from research. At the final seance, conducted at a New York hotel suite, Elvis's surprised relatives confessed they saw him pace the room, heard his laughter, and were struck, word after word, by the mannerisms and peculiar mood changes so characteristic of the Elvis they knew in life. The range of emotions displayed during the seance drained all of us and left Dorothy, our medium, shaken and crying as she passed on the emotionally charged words of the star.

The room seemed filled with electricity as a candle was lit in front of a simple photograph of Elvis. Shortly after Dorothy had relaxed sufficiently to allow the spirit of Elvis to impress her, the seance got underway. Within moments, the tense expression on the family's faces turned to shocked surprise as the medium established direct contact with the singer. It was obvious that he recognized them, even though Dorothy had no idea who Dee or David were. Through the medium Elvis made it clear he understood the historic significance of this confrontation, to prove his true identity from the beyond and to get his messages across. As I watched the usually placid face of Dorothy Sherry change to a near-likeness of Elvis, who now controlled her, statements came from Elvis in rapid succession that left no doubt about his identity and actual presence in our midst.

He told of a private conversation he had had with his bodyguard, David Stanley, just a few days before his death. "I'll take care of you, even if I'm not here," Elvis told the young man who had grown up in his home and who traveled with Elvis, charged with protecting the singer. He revealed intricate details of the Las Vegas Hilton hotel, where he often performed. Dorothy Sherry has never been to Las Vegas. He spoke of David's career goals, his love for cameras, and his desire to be an actor. Since Dorothy never met David Stanley before the seance, and had no idea who he was when she entered the room, there is no way she could have acquired such intimate knowledge.

He mentioned the nights they had spent singing gospel songs in hotel rooms and how they alternated between high-pressured worries and mad laughter during those cross-country tours. None of this was public knowledge. He revealed to Dee Presley his concern over past, unpublicized death threats to his daughter and expressed his deep feelings of guilt again and again over neglecting her while in the body. He directed a message to Dee concerning the anxious last phone call made after a traumatic argument in a previous call strained their relationship. It was a call made the day he died, and nobody but Dee would have known of it, certainly not Dorothy.

He admitted to having been a psychic healer, stating that on one occasion he had healed the injured leg of a friend. According to David Stanley the incident was authentic, though neither it nor Presley's healing power were ever known publicly.

He revealed at the seance that he was in a state of total paranoia just before his passing, deeply concerned about his security and threats against his life—a fact only Stanley and a handful of intimates knew. He used the exact words he told bodyguard Stanley two days before he died: "I'll take care of you, I'll be around." He displayed an intimate knowledge of Stanley's career goals, including his thoughts of being a photographer and frantic desire to be as famous as his idol—facts readily admitted afterward by the young man.

As tears streamed down the medium's face, Elvis spoke of his fears and anxieties, his great concern at being alone after his mother's death, a side of the star never shown in public and known only to his closest relatives and friends.

Practically before Dorothy was entranced, Elvis asked for Charley. He was very concerned over Charley Hodge, a musician and close friend of the singer, whose depression over Elvis's death had worried David Stanley so much that he was in almost daily contact with him the week before the seance.

He brought up his interest in reincarnation and the many conversations he and David had had on this subject. He described in great detail his palatial home, Graceland, mentioned his grandmother and two favorite pieces of jewelry—all of it corresponding to the facts. He spoke of his mother, now with him in the spirit world, and her weakness, while in the flesh, concerning alcohol, a fact that has never been publicized for obvious reasons but that, according to the family, is nevertheless entirely accurate.

The relatives came away from the seance convinced that Elvis had been present. David Stanley confessed he "heard his laughter" the way only Elvis would laugh; Dee Presley felt his anger rising like a physical force—precisely the way it was when the singer was still alive in this world. The medium complained of being practically burned with searing heat and trembling with anger, but was unable to understand why. Dee Presley, however, understood.

When the seance ended, Dorothy, still in a state of great agitation, asked for a glass of water. She felt hot and shaky, a state she had never been in after a trance before. As soon as her equilibrium was restored, I escorted her to the elevator and then returned to the suite.

David Stanley, who had initially been negative toward the entire encounter, was now a changed man. He readily confirmed many of the things that had been said through Dorothy's mediumship, and added that he himself had actually realized that Elvis was pacing up and down behind him, just as Dorothy had claimed. As for Dee Presley, her strict religious outlook made it difficult for her to accept spirit communication outside the religious establishment, and she was frank in admitting she did not "believe in" reincarnation, a cardinal point in Elvis' message and continued existence on the Other Side. Despite this, she was visibly impressed with what had just transpired in her presence. "That phone call," she kept saying to us, "if she could only get more about that telephone call—when it was made, and under what circumstances." I promised Dee I would ask Dorothy to convey this request to Elvis if he should come to her that night.

The following morning, July 15, Dorothy called me in great agitation. "I've got your answer," she said, explaining that Elvis was pleased with our seance, but at the same time frank in admitting he had been extremely agitated by the presence of two family members: the stepbrother, close friend, and bodyguard with whom he had shared so much of his life, and the stepmother who knew so much of his personal dilemma. But, Dorothy told me on the telephone, there had been a lot of anger and fighting between Elvis and Dee—he had resented the marriage of his father's at first, feeling it had come too soon after his mother died."

But what about the telephone call, I pressed. Under what circumstances was it made? "It's connected with a doctor . . . an ambulance . . . the house," Dorothy replied.

The truth of the matter is this: there were two telephone calls that last day of Elvis's life on earth. The first one was a consuming, heated argument between himself and his stepmother. The second one, moments before his passing, was an attempt to smooth things over again between them. Only Dee knew this, and, of course, Elvis.

But Dorothy could not understand why Elvis had come to her. His explanation that she would be believed because she was just a psychic housewife did not satisfy her. Finally Elvis admitted that he knew, from where he now existed, that he and Dorothy had been together in an earlier lifetime. It was a bond that apparently transcended the grave.

XVIII

THE STRANGE CASE OF THE PSYCHIC CALL GIRL

had never expected to be called in for help with unwanted ghostly lovers by a call girl—but there I was listening to Lily's "complaint."

"I remember the night I was conceived. My father was having intercourse with my mother and she was complaining that he was hurting her. Ever since, I felt angry at my father for hurting my mother," Lily said, and threw her head back in a gesture of defiance.

Lily was then twenty-nine, with incredibly large, beautiful eyes.

Lily is probably the only psychic call girl in the world. We were sitting in her East Side apartment on one of Manhattan's more expensive streets. The apartment was well furnished in a sort of nonchalant, modern way. There was nothing ostentatious or vulgar about either the apartment or Lily. There were landscape paintings on the walls, and through the windows you could look out onto still another one of those modern, expensive apartment houses of which there are so many on

New York's East Side. There were thick curtains in front of the windows that could be drawn when necessary.

I met Lily a month before when she was in trouble, real serious trouble. Not the trouble call girls can get into sometimes, but the kind psychics can get into if they are not careful. Lily came to see me because she did not know how to cope with the undead, the spirits of those who kept bothering her night after night until she could no longer sleep.

I was somewhat taken aback by her initial remarks. "What do you mean, you saw yourself being conceived?" I asked "Where exactly were you? I mean, from what vantage point did you see the scene?"

"From inside."

As a parapsychologist and psychic investigator, I was familiar with cases of people seeing their bodies below while floating above, but this was a little different.

"Did you ever tell your parents about it?"

"No. They wouldn't understand."

Lily was born in Manhattan, the child of an Italian truck driver. She has an older sister and the family lived in a flat on the Lower East Side at the time. From the very beginning, Lily was a strange child.

"When I was only a year old, I tried to communicate with my parents without using my mouth," Lily explained, "but they didn't understand. I tried to communicate with them *through my eyes*. Years later I learned about telepathy. I recalled a previous life and tried to tell my parents, but of course I couldn't."

Lily has always felt "strange" and somehow out of place in her present body, and she longs to "go home" but doesn't know where home is.

I knew, of course, that Lily's "work" was sex, but I

was not quite prepared for her out-of-the body flights and psychic phenomena. But then again, this is not altogether unusual: sex and ESP do go together, because they originate in the same place. Parapsychology has long recognized the close relationship between sexual energies and the power to break through the time and space barrier. The plexus at the top of the head and the solar plexus in back of the stomach—both highly sensitive ganglia of nerves—are also considered the focal points of psychic energy. The whitish substance exteriorized occasionally by physical mediums during experiments and commonly called "ectoplasm" is closely related to sexual fluid; in my view it replaces the secretion of that fluid when the subject is unable to express his or her sexual drive satisfactorily. This can lead to physical manifestations called poltergeist phenomena, during which objects move about seemingly by their own volition but actually through the power of psychokinesis, "mind over matter."

Nobody could accuse an active call girl of suppressing her sexual drive—at least on the face of it. Only when I learned that she does her "work" totally separated from her *emotional* self did I realize why Lily was having all that psychic trouble: satisfying all those clients in bed in no way satisfied her emotional needs.

Coming from a strict home, Lily did not have sex until she was seventeen, and the following year she fell madly in love with a boy named Eric. After an Andy Warhol movie Eric took her to his apartment in Brooklyn and made love to her.

"I knew at that moment I was pregnant . . . I felt it. He wanted me to have an abortion, but I refused. I can't kill anything."

When it was clear that Eric could not be counted on to marry Lily, her parents did everything to lose the baby. Despite her deep depression, she was forced to go to work. Her parents drove her to the station every morning and made sure she got on the train to the city, and as soon as she got back, instead of letting her rest, they forced her to walk up and down to make sure she would lose the baby. When she began to bleed and suffer the deepest agony of body and soul, her parents rejoiced; they took it to be a sign she would soon lose the baby, and so she did.

"They killed it—I understood what they were doing but I had no power because I was so weak at the time and I never forgave them for that."

The pain was excruciating, but her parents forced her to return to work a week later. A few weeks passed, and Lily went about her job barely conscious of what she was doing. One day, as she was returning from work on the subway, a group of neighbor girls joined her to give her the news. Hadn't she heard? About Eric?

"What about Eric?" Lily replied, used by now to the fact that the whole neighborhood knew. But this had nothing to do with her pregnancy. This was different. Eric had been in a car accident on his way back to California. He was on the critical list. The news hit her hard. She left her body and felt herself floating above it through the subway car. Luckily, one of her girlfriends grabbed her body to keep it from sagging to the floor. Somehow, she made it home. That night, Eric died in the hospital, but Lily didn't know it. As she lay in bed, she suddenly felt a powerful pull in her navel. The next moment, she saw Eric enter her room and kiss her good-bye. She saw him with her psychic eye and he looked as beautiful to her then as he always had. When she got to the wake, however, she couldn't recognize him; the accident had badly mangled the body.

Several weeks later the family moved again. Slowly, Lily returned to normal. The apartment was to Lily's liking, she had her own room now. One night, shortly after their arrival, she was busy sewing curtains, her father and her brother were out for the evening, and her mother was in her own room. All of a sudden Lily felt a cold, cold draft and as she looked up to find out what was happening, she heard her mother call out from the other end of the apartment, "Lily, did you just pass my room?" But Lily hadn't budged. The cold had now entered her room and gripped her with icy claws. Suddenly she saw that a figure had entered her room. At first it was hazy but then she recognized Eric. Frightened, Lily ran out of her room and into her mother's. Her mother was as white as the wall. She, too, had sensed a presence, although she had not seen him. After that visit, Lily refused to sleep in her room and slept instead on a couch in the living room. One night she and her brother decided to use the ouija board. Quick as a flash, it spelled E-R-I-C.

About that time she met Ian at a coffee shop. "He was raggy looking, about twenty-six years old, and I just knew this one was for me. Something told me I'd have a long relationship with that stranger, and so I did!"

One night, when she left his place in a hurry, she forgot to put her nylons back on; her mother noticed it and called her a tramp. The following morning she packed her bags and left home. She had just turned twenty and there was a lot of world out there waiting for her.

She was ready to move in with Ian but he would have none of it, so she went to live with a girl named Helen. "Ian would come over and we would play games. I would leave my body, and I saw myself, glowing, and I looked out the window and everything around me was like a doll house, beautiful and radiant. I had the feeling I could do anything, feel anything, pure feeling being in control of everything. Eventually I came back into my body, but I'll never forget that experience."

One night she and a girlfriend experimented with regression. She would go into a trance state and retrace her steps "as far back" as she could, always keeping in mind to identify herself with any previous lives. Retracing her time track, she suddenly stopped at an even two thousand years ago. That's when she discovered that Ian was really Jesus reincarnated and she, Lily, was Mary Magdalene. Naturally, she knew all about the crucification. "I know it was a plot. A plot to make people believe that it wasn't supposed to end up that way. Jesus was not supposed to be killed but it was all to make those ignorant people understand you have to make things mysterious. The plot didn't work."

Then Lily found a job as a hatcheck girl in a lesbian nightclub on Third Avenue. The place was high-class and belonged to a lesbian and a straight man named Joe. Joe evidently had a good eye for hatcheck girls.

"The first night he saw me, he put money in my hand and said, 'I'll see you later.' I didn't understand what he meant, I was so naive. I called my girlfriend and she said, 'Lily, he wants to see you.' "

That night, after the club closed, she made her first thirty-five dollars in the "world's oldest profession."

With her professional career launched in earnest, Lily decided to enjoy her work.

Despite her new career, however, she was very much attached to Ian. It was a year since he had left her, but she kept dreaming of him. "One night when I wanted him especially badly, I had gone to bed in a funny kind of mood. I couldn't fall asleep . . . something kept making me restless. Finally I drifted off. It must have been hours later, in the middle of the night, when I woke up. There at arms length I saw the shadow of a man, all white, like a snowman . . . and he was on top of me, making love to me! I felt pressure on my legs . . . and I went right along with it . . . enjoying it . . . and I cried out, 'Ian! Ian!' but as soon as I had acknowledged his presence, the white figure rolled up into a little ball and disappeared in a flash!"

Astral sex is by no means impossible nor unique, I explained to Lily. Ian might not even have been aware of his "trip" because the unconscious can do funny things quite on its own. Lily's emotional message could have triggered the long-distance reaction. If Lily needed further proof of her mediumship, the strange state of total *emotional* exhaustion—even though her emotions were in no way involved in her "work"—was the answer. She felt exactly the way a physical medium feels after a heavy seance!

Word of mouth had it that Lily was not like any other call girl, but something unique. Soon she had more clients than she could handle and so she became very selective. Again, her sixth sense told her whom to see and whom to avoid. Whether it was her wider use of her psychic powers, or just the fact that she felt financially secure and comfortable in her clean, new home,

Lily's psychic experiences began to take on new dimensions. At night she begin to see what she thought were molecules or uncertain shapes, and she took them to be spirits wishing to communicate with her or through her.

"A few nights later I suddenly found myself in a strange state of trance. I couldn't wake up, yet I observed everything going on around me. I couldn't move, no matter how much I tried. Then, suddenly, I felt something heavy on top of me . . . someone invisible was pressing on me. . . . It was definitely a human body, and there was no mistaking its intention. In a second I realized that a ghostly male was having intercourse with me . . . and even more amazing, I was actively participating. It felt . . . well, just like having sex with a man, only I couldn't see anything. But I sure felt it."

The next morning she told herself that she had only had a sex dream, but when the experience returned the following night she knew that she wasn't dreaming.

"I could see the room clearly, but I couldn't move. My body was paralyzed, yet someone was having sex with me at the same time. I could feel the weight of his body on top of me, there was no mistaking it."

I explained to Lily what the problem was: being a call girl, a lover-for-pay, without emotions involved, allowed those emotional energies she seemed to possess in such large amounts to go untapped, until sexually hungry spirits discovered her. I did what I could to close her psychic "door," as it were, and having heard nothing further from her must assume she has come to terms with her ghostly lovers, one way or another.

XIX

THE FIANCÉ
WHO WOULDN'T
GIVE UP

Unfortunately it sometimes happens that an engagement to marry remains unfulfilled because one of the partners dies. Knowing that they may be together again in the future when the other partner passes on, though spiritually rewarding, is not realistically helpful. When one of the two lovers or marriage-partners-to-be is unwilling to accept this transition and continues to try to reach out to his or her surviving partner in the physical world, there are bound to be problems, especially if the surviving partner does not welcome such attentions.

There are cases on record where the lover who has gone on cannot quite manage a physical presence or even an apparition, but chooses—or is forced—to resort to using the physical body of his love partner to manifest, either through automatic writing, some form of temporary possession, or even the movement or placement of objects in the house to somehow convey a message.

Virginia F. is an average person of full Irish descent, as she describes herself—of "the black Irish," those who think they are related to the Spanish Armada survivors who took refuge in Ireland in 1588 and later intermingled with the native population. Mrs. F. has five children and lives in a modest home in one of the largest cities of New England. The house was built in February 1955 and sold to a Mr. and Mrs. J. S. Evidently the home was far from lucky for the first owner, whose wife died of cancer in it after about four years. The next owners were C. and E. B. Within a year of acquiring the house they filed for a divorce. A short time later, their oldest son was run over and killed by a truck. At that point, the house passed into the hands of Mrs. F. and her family. A little over two months after they had moved in, her father had a heart attack in the bathroom and died on the way to the hospital. For nine years Mrs. F. and her family managed to live in the house, but their marriage was not a happy one, and it ended in a divorce in 1970. Whether or not the tragic atmosphere of the house has any bearing upon what transpired later is hard to tell, but Mrs. F. thought enough of it to advise me of it and I'm inclined to think that the depressing atmosphere of a house may indeed lead to psychic complications. It could very well be that an earlier dwelling stood on the same spot and that some of the older vibrations are clinging to the new house.

On May 25, 1970, Mrs. F.'s divorce was complete. In the fall of the same year she met another man. Francis and his sister Gloria had visited the house after a club meeting, and from that moment on Mrs. F. and the new man were inseparable. It was love at first sight. For a few weeks the two went everywhere together, and then the happiness came to a sudden end. Francis was ill with an incurable disease. He knew he had not long to live. Instead of a wedding, she helped plan his funeral. The night before he died, he told her he would never leave her and that nothing and no one could ever separate them. He also told her that he would come for her soon. That night he died. And when he died his electric clock stopped exactly at the moment he passed out of the body. For the last day of his life Francis was attended day and night by Mrs. F. and her two sons, but nothing could be done to save him.

When the man knew that his time was short, he started to talk with her about death and what he wanted to be done. She had promised to buy the lot in the cemetary next to his; faithful to his request, the day after she had buried him, February 14, 1972, she bought the lot.

That day, strange things started to happen in her home. There was first of all a picture that Francis had bought for her, showing the Minutemen on the Lexington Green. The picture would actually fly off the wall, no matter how many times she refastened it. Several times the picture actually flung itself across the room, making a terrific noise. During the three days between Francis's death and his burial, a little valentine she had given him in the hospital was moved by unseen hands. Someone took it from a ticket to which it was fastened by a paper clip and turned it around so that the side on which was written "Love G." was on top. But no one in the house had done it.

The day of the funeral, Mrs. F. fell asleep, exhausted from the emotional upset. At four o'clock in the morning she woke up to find written on a piece of paper near her the words "Remember, I love you, Francis."

Realizing that this message had somehow come through her hands even though she was unaware of it, she tried consciously to receive another message by automatic writing. The first line consisted of scribbled letters that made no sense whatsoever. But the second line became clearer. It was a love message written in the handwriting of the deceased. There was no mistaking it.

When she confided to her family doctor, he shook his head and prescribed sedatives. In her heartbroken state, Mrs. F. remembered how her fiancé had promised her a pearl ring for Christmas but had been too sick then to buy it. The matter of the missing pearl ring had been a private joke between them. Two days after the last automatic message, she was putting some things away in the bedroom of her house. Carefully she cleaned the top of her dresser and put everything in its proper place. A short time later her oldest daughter asked her to come up to the bedroom. There on the dresser was a pearl. How had it gotten there?

"Do these things truly happen, or am I on the verge of a breakdown?" Mrs. F. asked herself. She remembered how she had written to me some years ago concerning some ESP experiences she had had. Again she got in touch with me, this time for help. "Help me, please, to understand. And if you tell me that I'm losing my mind," she wrote, "then I'll go to the hospital." But if I assured her that she was not insane, she would fight. All she really wanted was to be with her Francis at this point.

Mrs. F. was indeed in a fix. There was nothing wrong with her love relationship, but Francis's promise to take her over to his side of life was another matter. I was convinced that those who were guiding him now would also instruct him accordingly. Gently I explained to Mrs. F. that love cannot fully bridge the gap between the two worlds of existence.

There is a time for them to be joined, but for the present she belonged to the world of the body and must continue to live in it as best as she could. When she accepted her true position and also renewed responsibility towards her children, the hold that the deceased had had upon her lessened. It was as if Francis had understood that his business had indeed been finished. The knowledge of his continued existence in another dimension was all he wanted to convey to his one and only love. That done, he could await her coming in due time in the conviction that they would be together without the shadow of possession between them.

XX

GETTING TOGETHER "THE NEXT TIME AROUND"

eincarnation is not, as some people think, a mystical Eastern belief in the transmigration of the soul, but a serious body of evidence capable of being researched and investigated in a scientifically valid fashion.

Love beyond the grave may work in exceptional cases where the energy and passions are so strong that a manifestation can occur in the physical sense. The majority of separated or thwarted lovers may have to be content with "coming back" in another lifetime and succeeding with the desired mate, presumably also reincarnated at the same period in time. In fact people frequently recognize each other when meeting for the first time as somehow having met before, though there is no hard evidence that they have. It is perhaps only a vague memory from another lifetime, if indeed it is a true sense of recognition and not just an easy ploy to start up a conversation with an attractive member of the opposite sex!

"The evidence indicates that reincarnation is a fact.

I think it likely that people have been born before and that after they die will be born again on this earth." This is the headline-making quotation in an article on reincarnation in the popular weekly the *National Enquirer*. This weekly newspaper is not known for its subtlety of approach, nor necessarily for the reliability of its information. But in recent times the *Enquirer* has concentrated on the field of parapsychology, astrology, and the occult in general. As a result, its circulation has risen to even greater heights than before.

The above quotation is not from some metaphysical believer, or astrologer, or amateur investigator. It is the opinion of Dr. Ian Stevenson, head of the Department of Neurology and Psychiatry at the University of Virginia's School of Medicine. Dr. Stevenson has for many years been the champion of reincarnation research in the United States. His first book on the subject, *Twenty Cases Suggestive of Reincarnation*, was soon followed by additional material published through the American Society for Psychical Research, and another book of additional cases is now in preparation. Stevenson has investigated cases in both the West and the East and has done so on a careful, scientific basis. No one can rightly accuse Dr. Stevenson of being a charlatan, or of jumping to conclusions. His language is careful and he makes no unjustified claims. The difficulty toward total acceptance of his findings, and the findings of others like myself, which parallel them, lies in the stubborn insistence on the part of most orthodox scientists that laboratory experiments are the only way of proving reincarnation. "Nobody has as yet thought up a way that reincarnation could be proved in a laboratory or a test tube," the professor is quoted in his interview. In studying hundreds of valid reincarnation cases he used the methods of the historian, lawyer, and psychiatrist in combination. Gathering testimony from as many witnesses as he could, he and his staff sometimes interviewed as many as twenty-five people regarding a certain case. Sometimes he returns for further interviews if the original talk has not been satisfactory or conclusive. Everything is taken into account: the behavior of the person who claims to have lived before, the environment in which he lives, his background, education, and general knowledge, and even his personal habits. "Many of those claiming to have lived before are children. Often they are very emotional when they talk of the person they used to be and they can give minute details of the life they lived," Dr. Stevenson added.

Dr. Stevenson, just as any responsible parapsychologist does, always looks for alternate explanations before he accepts reincarnation as the answer to a puzzling case. Everything is considered: early experiences, accidental information, newspaper accounts, anything that might have been forgotten consciously but can be brought out under hypnosis. Fraud, memory lapses, fantasy, and wishful thinking have all got to be considered and eventually ruled out before a valid case for reincarnation can be established, according to Dr. Stevenson's method of inquiry. But that is by no means the end. He explained that he must also consider and exclude telepathy as a means of obtaining unusual information. "Extrasensory Perception cannot account for the fact that the subject has skills and talents not learned, such as the ability to speak a foreign language without having had the opportunity to learn it in this present life."

Although most of the cases investigated by Dr. Stevenson were in India and the East, he has also looked into some interesting situations in Alaska and Europe. This is not because fewer cases occur in the West, but because the prevailing attitude of the public makes discovery of such cases more difficult. In the East, the climate is more favorable toward a free and open discussion of such matters; in the West only very courageous people dare come out with statements that they may have lived before.

The author of the *Enquirer* article, Doug Laurie, then asked Dr. Stevenson whether reincarnation might not explain child geniuses such as Wolfgang Amadeus Mozart or Alexander Hamilton. Mozart was an accomplished musician and composer before the age of ten; Alexander Hamilton had almost no formal education, yet could speak French fluently before the age of twelve. Dr. Stevenson allowed that the incidence of child genius cases might be attributable to reincarnation.

The article then quoted in some detail half a dozen cases investigated by Dr. Stevenson and by his colleague Dr. H. N. Banerjee of India, all of them completely proven in every detail. Those among my readers who wish to acquaint themselves with these verified cases of reincarnation may find lengthy accounts of the investigations in the books of Dr. Stevenson and Dr. Banerjee.

New evidence and new cases suggesting reincarnation turn up constantly. The *New York Daily News* of January 9, 1971, told of Alfonsito Weshner, age four, as the star of discussions with college professors in Montreal. "Alfonsito amazed the educators with general knowledge and his special interests music and the arts."

Old-line scientists prefer to regard reincarnation

research as exotic and reject the evidence out of hand without ever examining it. Some parapsychologists, even conservative ones, are eager to examine what material there is, especially since Dr. Stevenson has opened the door to such investigations. The acceptance of reincarnation as a reality is a hard nut to swallow for some. Inevitably it means simultaneous acceptance of survival after physical death. Some parapsychologists still cannot accept that probability, simply because they have been weaned on laboratory research methods and cannot or do not wish to understand that the evidence is in the *field,* among spontaneous phenomena or actual, unplanned occurrences.

The material for the survival of human personality is overwhelming, far more so than the evidence for reincarnation. Strangely, though, some support for reincarnation research can be gotten among scientists who, on the surface, seem the least likely to be interested in such a subject. I am speaking here of physicists and physical scientists. The reason is that in learning about the nature of energy and mass, and in dealing with the electromagnetic forces in the universe, many of these scientists have come to realize that energy is indestructible. Basing their views to some extent on Albert Einstein's pioneering opinions, they, too, feel that energy may be transformed into other forms of power or into mass, but can never be dissipated entirely. Since the life force, the human personality, is an energy field, they argue that such fields cannot be dissipated either and must therefore *continue to exist in some form.* Experiments involving the discovery of energy fields in so-called haunted locations and of significant changes in the atmosphere of an experimental chamber, such as ionization, have been going on for some time. It is therefore not too surprising that such strong centers of technical learning as the Newark College of Engineering and the New York Institute of Technology (where I teach) should be interested in parapsychology, and within that field, reincarnation research.

Medical science has been more hostile toward reincarnation material than any other branch of science. This may be due to the fact that medical science relies heavily upon the assumption that man is essentially a physical being. As Dr. William McGary, the brilliant physician working in conjunction with the Association for Research and Enlightenment in Phoenix, Arizona, has pointed out to me, the basic difference between orthodox medical science and medicine based upon such knowledge as the Edgar Cayce records lies in the way they regard the human being. To conventional medicine, man is structural, that is to say, the physical body is the essence of man and mind is merely a subdivision thereof. To the esoterically oriented person, man is functional, not structural. The physical person is a manifestation of spirit or mind that came first, and represents the outward expression of the soul that governs and determines everything from within. Such thinking is at variance with conventional medical procedure, of course, since it necessitates the treating of illness from a total point of view rather than from the usual sectional or physical viewpoint.

For a medical doctor to accept reincarnation as a reality necessitates changes in his medical approach as well; except for the psychiatrist, the conventional physician has little to do with the nonphysical aspects of human personality. The general practitioner and the specialist both leave mental problems to the psychiatrist, concentrating on purely physical problems. Thus the question of reincarnation research becomes essentially one of acceptance or rejection by the psychiatrist and psychoanalyst. Today, the majority of psychiatrists explain any valid reincarnation material as malfunctions of personality, ranging all the way from mild neuroses to schizophrenic conditions. Just as the conventional analyst will regard *all* dream material of his patient as purely symbolic and representative of suppressed material in the unconscious part of the mind, so the psychiatrist will explain reincarnation memories either as aberrations of the mind, or, if the particular psychiatrist is a Jungian, as racial memories or archetypes.

But these scoffing psychiatrists and analysts seem to forget that Dr. Sigmund Freud, the father of modern psychiatry, himself leaned toward parapsychology in the later years of his life. He made the statement in print that he would want to study parapsychology if he had to do it all over again. One of his star pupils, Dr. Carl Jung, who has contributed as much to psychiatry as Freud, was not only firmly convinced of the reality of psychic phenomena but possessed ESP himself. His discovery, or if you prefer, invention of the *archetypes* as a symbolic expression of "original concepts" does not, in his view, militate against genuine reincarnation experiences. At the Jung Institute in Zurich, much research went on in this area in the 1930s and 1940s. In his important work *Synchronicity: An Acausal Connecting Principle,* Jung postulates that there is a superior order of things connecting events and people. This superior order lies beyond the law of cause and effect and must be dealt with on different terms. What Jung is hinting at in this precedent-shaking work is the existence of a law of fate; by trying to explore the ways in which this non-causal link seemed to work, Jung approached the question of fate, free will, and reincarnation, which is intimately connected with them in a modern, scientific way for the first time.

Some years ago, the late Eileen Garrett, world-renowned medium and president of the Parapsychology Foundation, accompanied Dr. Robert Laidlaw, psychiatrist and head of a department of psychiatry at Roosevelt Hospital, New York City, to a number of mental institutions in order to discover whether some of the inmates might be suffering from genuine cases of possession. The very fact that a reputable medical doctor would even attempt to undertake such an expedition is an incredible step forward. Dr. Laidlaw never made any claims of wholesale acceptance of the tenets of parapsychology. But he did accept that which, in his view, had been proven without reservations. He engaged himself in research dealing with psychical healing and has shown a great deal of interest in cases of hauntings and ESP in general. It was Dr. Laidlaw who conducted the investigation with me when the late *New York Daily News* columnist Danton Walker invited us to his haunted house in Rockland County. Laidlaw has an open mind on reincarnation; he is actively working with the American Society for Psychical Research and other bodies in accumulating facts pertaining to reincarnation that may yield a better understanding of the system by which it works.

In the spring of 1973 I obtained permission to visit a lady named Verna M. in a state hospital in Georgia. She had been in and out of mental hospitals, confined generally as a case of schizophrenia. For some time prior to my visit, she had maintained that she remembered previous lifetimes. It was her contention that a full exploration of those earlier existences might help her understand her present predicament. I was her last hope, and even though she knew that I wasn't likely to come to central Georgia just to see her, she wrote to me in great despair. Apparently she was rational most of the time, lapsing at certain intervals into fits of schizophrenia and refusing to cope with life on the outside. At such times she was committed to, or voluntarily committed herself to, medical supervision.

It so happened that I had some business in Atlanta and arranged with Mrs. M. to visit her at the state hospital. Obtaining permission and even cooperation of the medical authorities at the state hospital was a remarkable accomplishment in itself. The institution turned out to be a modern, well-kept mental facility in rural central Georgia. The therapists and the supervising medical doctor greeted me with great cordiality.

I proceeded to interview Mrs. M., first in order to ascertain the details of her conscious memories. I was able to find certain inconsistencies in her narrative, inasmuch as reincarnation as an explanation was concerned. I discovered, for instance, that she had had a number of valid ESP experiences and also that she very definitely suffered from personality problems. Under hypnosis, which was undertaken by me on a kind of stage so that it could be taped for internal television, Mrs. M. proved to be an excellent subject and rapidly went to the third stage of hypnosis. I was able to discover some suppressed material concerning her own father, and other details that had not been known to the hospital authorities. Prenatal regression yielded nothing. But through hypnosis I discovered that the entity Mrs. M. had thought was *herself* in a previous incarnation was in fact a discarnate individual who had attached herself to Mrs. M. in order to continue expressing herself. Thus the supposed case of reincarnation turned out to be one of possession.

Upon bringing her out of her hypnotic state, I explained some of this to Mrs. M. and, as a result, she learned to accept conditions in her life as they are, no longer relying on previous incarnations and unfulfilled hopes as crutches that eliminated the need to stand on her own two feet in *this* life. Mrs. M. has since left the institution and returned to private life.

Whether or not conventional scientists will accept reincarnation research in the foreseeable future, the work will go on with even greater emphasis as time passes. Even in Russia, studies in reincarnation are now being undertaken. The rate of progress in the Western world will depend on the availability of trained investigators, good hypnotists, and of course good research facilities to back up the investigators. There is no dearth of promising subjects; the small selection mentioned in this work should give an indication of the available material. However, people without overt memories or other substantial indications of previous lives should not be put under hypnosis merely in the hope of finding previous lives. If reincarnation research were to be based solely on hypnotic regression, the outlook would indeed be grim. Even Dr. Ian Stevenson does not regard regression through hypnosis as the major factor in his research. As the initiator of reincarnation research, this technique is frequently useless and sometimes deceiving, but as a follow-up method it is valuable and frequently yields excellent results. Spontaneous, unsought occurrences are still the backbone of all valid reincarnation material.

XXI

SOUL MATES

Whenever two people are so attracted to each other that their relationship seems perfect and natural all around, they wonder if they are perhaps soul mates—destined by fate to come together because they are two halves of the same unit.

The theory behind the existence of soul mates goes back to the earliest history of mankind. Even in the "Old Religion" of the Stone Age a prime motivation to lead a good and useful life was the possibility of being reborn near the loved one in the next incarnation. In medieval times, the idea of the divinely joined couple runs through many romantic narratives. The German poet Johann Wolfgang Goethe wrote a novel called *Die Wahlverwandtschaften* ("elective affinities," or relationships by choice). It was his contention that every human being had a perfect mate waiting to be discovered. Goethe expressed in poetic form a philosophy that is perhaps the deepest and most significant element of all esoteric teachings.

At the beginning, it is thought, the soul was created

as an exterior expression of the Godhead, a unit unto itself and therefore neither male nor female, but both. Sometime in great antiquity the soul was split into a male and a female half and sent forth into the world to prove itself. Through testing and purification, the two halves were forever striving to reunite. In the process, the dynamics of the world were achieved. As a new result, a vastly strengthened and purified double soul would emerge, to become, perhaps, what the philosopher Nietzsche called Superman.

Since the soul mates were originally part of a larger unit, they would be possessed of knowledge that need not be explained from one to the other. Consequently one of the earmarks of finding the true soul mate was immediate recognition, instant understanding and communication beyond logical explanation, even beyond telepathy, accompanied by deep feelings of mutual love. The longing of one soul mate for the other is, in the eyes of the esoteric, the major driving force that makes man search the universe for fulfillment. Only by reaching out to this ideal soul mate can he hope to accomplish his destiny. It does not follow that everyone of us finds the destined soul mate, but the act of reaching is the important thing. By that very longing, the dynamic force of motivated desire is set into motion, and the multitude of such desires creates the power reservoir whence creative people obtain their inspirations and driving force.

Soul mates are not only physically attuned to each other and consequently perfect for each other in the sexual sense, but they share mutual interests, have identical outlooks on all phases of life, and are in every respect compatible. Soul mates are not necessarily ideal mates in terms of contemporary standards; they may differ greatly in age, social or economic background, or even race. As a matter of fact, some soul mates may be so radically different in outer appearance that the proof of their relationship lies in overcoming their differences rather than in accentuating them. But soul mates are always one male and one female, for there is no reference to homosexuality in esoteric philosophy.

But soul mates are by no means one of a kind. Every one of us has several potential soul mates, though he or she may never meet up with any of them. From the material I have investigated, and the philosophies I am familiar with, it would appear that each case is different and each personality requires a different set of circumstances and number of soul mates to find the whole self again. Some individuals may do so with one perfect soul mate. Some people will find such soul mates and actually marry them. The majority rarely do, but those who are esoterically awake will continue to hope that someday they will meet their soul mates, even though they may be married to someone else at the time. This, of course, creates another set of problems. If they find their perfect soul mates, should they abandon their conventional mate? If they do, they may find happiness but society may condemn them. If they do not, they will live with a sense of frustration to the end of their physical days.

Those who have the potential of uniting with several soul mates in their lives, usually the leaders of this world, the creative people, those who have much to give to the world, find one or several of these potential soul mates as they move through the years. For them to deny themselves the opportunity to unite with them, if only for a limited period of time, would cut off the free flow of the very energies they need to continue their mission on earth.

One has to be sure that the other person is truly a soul mate and that physical desires do not create a mirage. Many are the tests by which a true soul mate is recognized. Above all, comparison of previously held knowledge about a number of subjects, possibly the question of whether both soul mates felt identical reactions toward each other at the same time, and possible reincarnation memories, should all be taken into consideration before a conclusion is reached. On the other hand, conventional social, moral, and religious considerations should be carefully avoided in judging such a relationship. Frequently, the very point of such an unusual relationship is that it must be *outside* convention. In overcoming one's fears of conventionality, one earns the right to unite with the other soul mate. If it is a question of a number of soul mates during a lifetime, both partners should realize that the union may be of a limited duration for a purpose: once that which was meant to be accomplished by their coming together again has been completed, they must each go their separate ways to unite with other respective soul mates to accomplish still other purposes meant for them as a means of fulfilling their destiny.

At times, a couple becomes involved one with the other without realizing that they are actually soul mates. In the course of time they discover that their relationship was not merely a physical or spiritual or emotional one, but has developed beyond the usual elements into a deeper relationship and one day they realize that they were soul mates and stem from a common source. In such cases, of course, it may well be that the couple stays

together to the end of their earthly lives, no longer seeking other soul mates. In realizing that each individual
may have more than one perfect soul mate to merge
with we should not understand this necessarily as an
invitation to a kind of esoteric polygamy, but merely one
of possibilities. The fact that a number of potentially
equal soul mates or combinations of soul mates are in
existence may also mean that a particular individual has
more than one chance to merge with a perfect partner,
under different circumstances but with equal results.
This is particularly important in cases where an unhappy love affair creates the false impression in one
partner that his life's purpose has been aborted and that
he will never find the same kind of love again. Remember, we are *all* unique, and at the same time, *nothing* in
the universe is unique. The uniqueness of self is repeated in myriads of wondrous ways throughout the
universe—equal, parallel, similar and yet not quite the
same.

Let us assume that two people meet, both of them
not free in the conventional sense, and that they discover a deep longing for each other, far beyond physical
or emotional desire. If they are esoterically inclined,
they may discover that they are soul mates. To become
one, a perfect union on all levels—physical, mental, and
spiritual—is not a question of simply indulging themselves. The joy of such unions lies not in recognizing
their previous relationship but in implementing the opportunity that so patently has come their way for a reason. They cannot afford to overlook the opportunity, to
offend fate. They do not only have the chance to unite
again as they were once united, they have the sacred
duty to do so in order to recharge their energies for

further accomplishments in tune with the patterns of destiny. Avoiding such relationships leads to individual unhappiness and will surely cause the two potential soul mates to slow their progress. Furthermore, they will each and individually face a parallel situation again at some time in the future, whether in the same incarnation or in the next one, and will again be tested as to their responsibilities and the maturity of their decisions. It is therefore inescapable that when such conditions are recognized as cases of soul mates, direct and positive action is taken by both partners to fulfill the manifest desire of destiny.

HOW TO DEAL WITH LOVE BEYOND THE GRAVE

*A*s I have said at the beginning of this book, man is a triple entity—body, mind, and spirit, or soul. All three elements must be in harmony for true fulfillment, and when one is less strongly expressed than the other two imbalance will result, with all the problems that inevitably creates. Ideally, then, one should strive to maintain an equal balance among the three elements, though not many can.

When a close relationship of a romantic or sexual kind (preferably both together) comes to an end because one of the two participants passes out of the physical world, the continuance of that relationship is usually impossible for obvious reasons. But as I have reported in these pages, there are quite a number of instances where the obvious difficulties are being overcome by sheer passion and life force in the "dead" partner, proving once again that "life" by no means ends at death's door. For the surviving lover this represents problems that need to be addressed. If the attentions from beyond the grave are welcome, or even actively encouraged, they will of course preempt any new relationship on the physical earth level. The choice is yours.

But if the continuing romantic or sexual incursions by the "dead" partner continue and are not welcome because a new relationship has been formed by the surviving half, then there is need to deal with it in an appropriate way. Obviously the partner in the spirit dimension will hear and see the partner in the physical world, and if the surviving partner addresses the other lover in a kind but firm manner to express the desire to discontinue the attempts at a relationship from Beyond, chances are the other person will abide by these wishes, for no one wants to stay where he or she is not wanted.

But then again there are cases where this will not do: the "dead" lover is so hung up on the physical relationship he or she will not listen to entreaties. In extreme cases, where it becomes a serious threat to a new relationship, an exorcism is in order. This is not a fanciful discourse by a learned clergyman with a supposed devil (a figment of the church's imagination), but a ritual request to let go of the entanglement and to go on to the next state of existence in peace and with love. I have conducted such rituals, usually successfully, and both parties found peace afterward in their own way, in their own world.

It is unwise to allow a romantically possessive and exclusive relationship to continue between people living in two different worlds, no matter how close they may have been before one of them passed over. On the other hand, a continuing friendship and love is not necessarily evil or even undesirable. In time the partner who has passed on will be reconciled to the separation, or will perhaps even return through the process of reincarnation that affects all of us in different ways, at different times, as is suitable to each and every individual.

The majority of properly researched communications between those on the "earth plane" and those who have gone on to the next state of existence occur either directly at times when this is possible, or perhaps even allowed by the laws of the "Other Side," or through an intermediary such as a medium or psychic reader, either amateur or professional. Proof of identity is always desirable, and when the communication is via a professional psychic, one should bear in mind that only precise, personal data is proof of identity—data that the discarnate communicator can and should provide through the medium. Especially when a less than psychically talented person delivers messages from a "John" or a "Mary" and nothing more, one should exercise prudence in accepting such material as genuinely from a loved one.

Physical death occurs to people at various times in their development, and sometimes the residue of energy remains unspent. Why this happens so differentially and unequally is a matter for philosophical speculation, or perhaps the better understanding of the laws of karma. In any event, when that happens, that person may want to use the remaining physical energies, now residing in that person's "inner body" but totally controlled by the surviving mind, to contact the loved one left behind in the physical world. Sometimes this pool of available energy is added to by energy drawn from the recipient, or from others in the vicinity, usually without their consent or even knowledge. It is important to know that such happenings are in their own context natural and not the work of devils or demons, as some fanatic religions or cults would have us believe.

In the final analysis, if we are to accept a Greater Scheme of Things than what our rational mind can grasp, we will also accept the separation of death between lovers as part of that scheme, painful though it may be to us as individuals. But it is wise to keep in mind that a continuing love or active physical relationship between a discarnate and an incarnate person holds back the development of the souls of both parties in their respective lives.

Remember, too, that the world into which all of us will pass eventually is not so far away nor so terribly different from this one, and that *life never ends*.